MARCH OF THE HEROES

Other books by Gary Jennings

March of the Heroes

The Folk Hero Through The Ages

by

Gary Jennings

**All the doings of mankind, their wishes,
fears, anger, pleasures, joys and varied
pursuits, form the motley subject of my book.
—Juvenal**

ASSOCIATION PRESS • New York

MARCH OF THE HEROES

Published by Association Press, 291 Broadway, New York, N.Y. 10007

International Standard Book Number: 0-8096-1895-8
Library of Congress Catalog Card Number: 75-9863

Library of Congress Cataloging in Publication
Jennings, Gary.
   March of the heroes.

   Includes index.
   SUMMARY: Follows the march of heroes from earliest antiquity to the present day, indicating how each of them has reflected the culture, society, and life-style from which he or she sprang.
   1. Biography—Juvenile literature.   2. Heroes— Juvenile literature.   [1. Biography.   2. Heroes. 3. Folklore]   I. Title.
CT107.J44   920'.02   75-9863
ISBN 0-8096-1895-8

PRINTED IN THE UNITED STATES OF AMERICA

FOR ROBIN
fledgling heroine,
with love

Contents

MARCH OF THE HEROES

To the Young Reader

Men are not great or heroic because they are faultless; they are great and heroic because they dare, suffer, achieve and serve.
—Hamilton Wright Mabie

I live near Mexico City, and in that city is a wide boulevard called the Paseo de la Reforma, more than eight miles long, bordered with lawns, flower beds, towering trees, and every few yards the stone or bronze statue of some Mexican hero or man of distinction. Some of these dead-and-gone heroes are still revered by the people who stroll along this boulevard. Some are long forgotten by all but historians. But the point is that I could fill an entire book describing just the heroes of this one country, and do it with no more effort than that involved in copying the inscriptions on their statues along the Reforma.

By the same token, every country in the world, every culture and society, even the smallest tribe, has men and women to admire and idolize for their great and noble exploits. Many of them, even some of the least known, are worth a whole book to themselves; and, indeed, some of them—King Arthur, for one—have been the subject of whole libraries of books.

In writing this book, my intent has been to follow the "march of

11

the heroes" from earliest antiquity down through the centuries to the present day; to show how different peoples in different times have had different sorts of heroes and heroines, and how each of them has reflected the culture, society and life-style from which he or she sprang. So, in order to keep this book small enough to lift and read, I have had to select from among the throng.

Even the dull-witted cave men of the Stone Age may have had an occasional hero—a prodigious hunter, perhaps, who brought down a saber-tooth tiger singlehanded and whom the tribe remembered and admired for years after a saber-tooth brought *him* down. But the cave men left no records, so we will never know. We are equally ignorant of the heroes of the earliest civilizations, which left no histories but broken flint tools, pieces of cooking pots, and the like. Not until writing was invented, and scribes began to scribble on clay or wax tablets, papyrus or parchment, was there any enduring record of the notable events of the time. Many of those first "history books" have survived to our day, sometimes in fragments, sometimes in considerable detail. And there have been thousands of other history books written since.

Before we go any further, let us agree on just what a hero is. Say "hero" to most people and they will visualize a bemedaled warrior, a knight on a white horse, an Old West sheriff. A good many heroes are undeniably brave, strong, valorous—the most crowded chapters in this book are those dealing with warriors and conquerors. But there are other kinds of heroes as well: the wise, the good, the self-sacrificing. Different dictionaries give differing definitions of "hero." For the standard of this book, however, I have chosen this from the *Oxford English Dictionary*:

> HERO: A man who exhibits extraordinary bravery, firmness, fortitude or greatness of soul, in any course of action or in connection with any pursuit, work or enterprise; a man admired and venerated for his achievements and noble qualities.

That definition I would alter slightly to read "man or woman" because history abound in heroines and I have included many of them in this book.

Another of my criteria in selecting the heroes and heroines was that they should embody an interesting story that you won't find in every other book. In every retelling of a well-known hero's life, I have tried to unearth and present new and sometimes surprising aspects of his doings. I have searched diligently for heroes who have long been forgotten outside their home country or even their home town.

I have taken care not to treat any of my heroes and heroines with slavish and uncritical adoration. As well as their virtues and exploits, I have tried to give a glimpse of their faults and failings, for many a hero had a flaw: laziness, self-interest, greed, cowardice or even downright wickedness.

Some of the characters in these pages you may find hard to accept as heroes at all—Chairman Mao Tse-tung of Communist China, for example. Other heroes of some particular era have later deservedly been consigned to oblivion or recognized for the villains they really were. Some did only one heroic deed in a lifetime of unremarkable other activities. Some did a heroic deed unintentionally, or even against their will. Some were manufactured heroes, "created by popular demand," as one historian has put it, "sometimes out of the scantiest materials . . . such as the apple that William Tell never shot, the ride that Paul Revere never finished."

Some of the men and women regarded as heroic in their own time would seem to us to be preposterous freaks or lunatics if they did the same "heroic" things today. Another historian has remarked that "a modern Ajax would occupy a booth in a side show of a circus; a Joan of Arc, wandering into General Headquarters with a tale about 'hearing voices,' would be sent to a psychological ward for observation."

I don't pretend to know everything there is to know about the heroes I have included here, any more than I know all the heroes that have ever existed in the world. I have cited the reasons why I chose the heroes I have chosen. Others have used other criteria. In 1903, a man named J. McKeen Cattell made a list of "the one thousand greatest men in history," picking them on the basis of how many lines of print were allotted to them in the encyclopedias of the time. His list was headed by these ten: Napoleon, Shakespeare, Mohammed, Voltaire, Francis Bacon, Aristotle, Goethe, Julius Caesar, Martin Luther and Plato—only three of whom appear in this book.

I will explain a couple of my omissions. My opinion is purely personal and human, which is to say fallible. I have not included fictional "heroes" of the sort that star in novels, plays, movies, comic books, etc.—though some of them may be worthy of emulation. Don Quixote, for example, was only an imaginary character, but he so captured the hearts of his countrymen that now, nearly four hundred years later, I suspect that many Spaniards believe him to have been a real person. Because he wasn't, he is only briefly mentioned in this book. However, Don Quixote's creator, Miguel Cervantes, in his lifetime had quite as many heroic adventures (and misadventures) as his "hero," so Cervantes does merit several pages.

You will find comparatively few sports heroes in this book, and those few mainly for heroic doings only incidentally connected with sports. I do not quite concur with Bernard Shaw's observation that "games are diversion for people who can neither read nor think." But I do believe, however, that sports achievements are so fleeting and forgettable that they aren't worth dwelling on. Can *you* name the team that won the World Series or the Super Bowl Game five years ago?

There may be among us, at this moment—as there have been in the past—unrecognized heroes who may forever go unrecognized. You yourself, wherever you live or have traveled, may have walked in their footsteps. After all, any poor and hungry man who gives his last crust of bread to a still poorer man is as great a hero as Alexander the Great—or should be—though the world may never hear of him.

In Mark Twain's wise and witty novelette, *Captain Stormfield's Visit to Heaven*, we are told how all of heaven's angels, archangels, cherubim and its whole population of souls turned out in a grand ceremony to welcome the arrival of the soul of a humble Tennessee tailor, how all heaven exerted itself to make up for the neglect and scorn which that man had suffered on earth, to lavish on him all the honors he had deserved in his lifetime, and never got. One soul explains it to Captain Stormfield:

"That tailor Billings wrote poetry that Homer and Shakespeare couldn't begin to come up to; but nobody would print it; nobody read it but his neighbors, an ignorant lot, and they laughed at it. He wasn't ever expecting to go to heaven, much less that there was going to be any fuss made over him, so I reckon he was a good deal surprised when the reception broke on him. Shakespeare walked backwards before that tailor from Tennessee, and scattered flowers for him to walk on, and Homer stood behind his chair and waited on him at the banquet."

The soul glances down at earth and adds, "I wish we could send them word. That Tennessee village would set up a monument to Billings then, and his autograph would outsell Satan's."

It is enough to make every one of us stop and think: Who am I to scorn or despise or be cruel to the least and meanest of beings, when that being may be a hero unacclaimed, and I, like others, too blind to see the radiance?

The Great Ancients

All these were honored in their generations,
and were the glory of their times.
—Ecclesiasticus

Among the earliest and greatest heroes of whom we have written record are those of the ancient Greeks. Actually, their heroes date from long before writing came to Greece. There is every likelihood that these heroes did once exist as real, live men and women, and did remarkable feats worth remembering and retelling. For a thousand years or more, their exploits were handed down by word of mouth from generation to generation, and each new storyteller embellished the tales with new and more spectacular adventures.

The poet Homer put many of these tales into two epic poems—the *Iliad* and the *Odyssey*—composed entirely in his head, not on paper. Though they comprised a staggering 28,000 lines apiece, other storytellers assiduously memorized them and retold them to breathless audiences. The telling (or acting-out) of each epic took some fifteen hours and might be spread over five days. Shortly after Homer's time or perhaps while the master poet was still alive—about eight hundred years before Christ—the Greeks adopted (and improved) the writing system of the Phoenicians. Immediately, either Homer

17

or his successors put the *Iliad* and *Odyssey* down in writing, and to this day these works are considered masterpieces of literature. Later, other poets, authors and playwrights—Pindar, Plato, Euripides—took stylus or quill in hand to celebrate still other heroes and events of Greece's history.

In other countries we know of heroes even earlier than those of the Greeks, but the Grecian heroes had the greatest impact on our western world. As Rome rose out of barbarism, it deliberately hastened its advance toward civilization by imitating the already refined culture of Greece, a course which included adopting the Greek gods and heroes (though Rome gave many of them new names). And the civilization which the Roman Empire spread over the ancient world is still reflected in many of our present-day customs, words and beliefs.

In discussing the "great ancients" in this chapter I shall employ the original Greek names of the gods and heroes. You may well be more familiar with their later Roman names. So, to prevent confusion, here is a brief listing:

GREEK	ROMAN		GREEK	ROMAN
Aineias —	Aeneas		Hera —	Juno
Aphrodite —	Venus		Herakles —	Hercules
Ares —	Mars		Hermes —	Mercury
Asklepios —	Aesculapius		Odysseus —	Ulysses
Athena —	Minerva		Poseidon —	Neptune
Hades —	Pluto		Zeus —	Jupiter
Hephaistos —	Vulcan			

Most or all of the ancient Greek heroes may once have been real, living persons who accomplished feats that were extraordinary, but at least believable and not supernatural. By the time the legends got set down in writing, however, they were full of incredible miracles, monsters and fairy-tale fantasy. Even to make sense of these legends, it is necessary to know something about the ancient Greek gods and goddesses, whose "heaven" was supposedly atop Mount Olympus.

The Greeks made their gods in their own image, which is to say "human," and which is to further say "imperfect at best." The gods and goddesses were immortal; they could fly, could change their shapes, become visible or invisible at will, sling thunderbolts, work wonders and do other such godlike things. But they were also gluttonous in their appetites, touchy about being ignored or insulted, and fiercely jealous of each other. They meddled in human affairs, sometimes helping, sometimes hindering; they were notoriously lax in their morals, often unfaithful to their own Olympian mates, and thought nothing of making a mortal man or woman, married or not, fall in love with them. Zeus, the king of the gods, despite having the goddess Hera for a queen, blithely mated with at least twelve other goddesses and nymphs, along with at least seven mortal women, fathering countless godly and "demigod" descendants.

Many of Greece's heroes were already demigods even before they began their heroic adventures, because of having been born of a god and a mortal mother or a goddess and a mortal father. They might be slain on earth, but their souls were presumed to go on living forever, either among the gods on Olympus or in the paradise of the Elysian Fields, or in the constellations of the sky. An ordinary man, born of parents who were both mere mortals, might show such heroic promise that an Olympian god would take a personal interest in him—often helping him to even greater achievements. Then, on the hero's death, the "guardian" god would ensure that he was elevated to the status of demigod. One such was Ajax. After his death he became the "tutelary hero" (what today we would call the "patron saint") of the island of Salamis, where a festival was celebrated in his honor every year for hundreds of years.

PERSEUS

Perseus, one of the very earliest of the Greek heroes, not only had a god for a father but he also had three of them for allies. His story begins so far back in the long ago that not even the ancient Greek chroniclers could put a date to it. There was a certain King Akrisios of Argos (one of the many small kingdoms, or rather city-states, that made up Greece in those days) who was told by an oracle that he would die at the hands of his grandson. So he made certain that he would have no grandson—by locking up his only daughter, Danaë, in a high brass tower and setting guards around it. She would never even see a man, let alone marry one and have children.

However, there was no hiding a lovely lass like Danaë from the roving eye of Zeus. In the form of a shower of gold, like a swirl of gilded snowflakes, Zeus swept in through one of the tower's high windows; then quickly changing into the form of a handsome young man, he wooed and won Danaë. Nine months later, Danaë baffled her guards and outraged her father by giving birth to a son, whom she named Perseus. King Akrisios could not coldbloodedly murder his own grandson, so he decided to let the sea do it for him; he locked Danaë and the infant Perseus in a large chest and set it adrift on the Mediterranean Sea.

Zeus saw to it that the chest came safely ashore on the island of Seriphos, where a kindly old fisherman took the castaways into his house, gave them a home and brought up Perseus as his own grandson. The boy grew into a good-looking, strong and brave young man. Meanwhile, Polydektes, the king of the island, had developed a passion for the still lovely Danaë, but she found his advances repulsive. So Polydektes determined to take her by force, although he knew he would first have to get rid of her protecting son.

Polydektes called Perseus before him and said, "My boy, you have the makings of a hero, and it's time you went questing for an adventure worthy of your valor. I have just the job for you. Go and bring me the head of the Gorgon Medusa and you will be famed and acclaimed throughout the world." Perseus, eager as any other lad to become a hero, could not resist such a challenge. He set out in a wandering sort of way, not really knowing what the Gorgon Medusa was, nor where to look. In a forest only a few miles from home, however, he met Athena, the goddess of wisdom; Hermes, the god of travelers; and Hades, the god of the underworld.

Said Athena: "That treacherous king did not tell you, Perseus, how many men have lost their lives to the three Gorgon sisters. Two are terrible enough, but the one called the Medusa has the power of turning to stone any man who looks on her face." Athena then lent to Perseus a metal shield polished to the brilliance of a mirror, and a sword so sharp it would cut through iron. Hermes lent him a pair of winged sandals that would whisk him in a trice to anywhere in the world, and Hades lent him a cap that would render him invisible. Perseus slipped on the sandals, thanked the three helpful gods, and bounded off in the direction Athena had indicated.

He soon came to the Gorgons' domain, to find the land studded with what appeared to be statues. These were men, women, and even animals who had met the Medusa face to face and had been turned to stone. Perseus found the Gorgons asleep in a cave, and quietly approached them—taking the precaution of walking backward and eying them in the mirrorlike surface of his polished shield. Two of the Gorgons appeared to be merely ugly women; the third, however, was a superbly beautiful young woman except that, instead of hair, she had a head of writhing, hissing snakes; that one had to be Medusa. Still employing the shield for a mirror, Perseus struck backhanded, and his sword severed her head at a single blow. Without looking at the head, he stuffed it into a leather sack and took to the air—just as the other two Gorgons awoke screeching and tried to seize him.

Perseus flew a roundabout way home, and at one point—perhaps on the coast of what is now Israel—he glanced down to see a lovely young maiden chained to a rock by the seaside. He alighted beside her and asked the reason for her predicament. Her name was Andromeda, she said, and she was the daughter of King Cepheus of this land, whose people worshipped the nymphs of the sea. Her vain mother, Queen Cassiopeia, had rashly boasted that she was more beautiful than any sea nymph, and this had angered Poseidon, the god of the sea. He had sent a horrible, flame-breathing sea serpent which made repeated raids along the coast, burning and devouring everybody within its reach. An oracle told King Cepheus that he would soon have no people left to rule unless he sacrificed his daughter to the beast, when Poseidon would be placated and call off the scourge.

At this moment here came the monster, churning in from the sea, its fiery breath making the water boil and steam around it. Perseus leaped to meet it—and the battle was on. The serpent was so encrusted with barnacles that even the magic sword had trouble piercing its hide, but Perseus was invisible to the thrashing dragon, and his winged sandals enabled him to dodge the eruptions of fire from its furnace mouth. After much effort, he managed to hack the beast so severely that it rolled belly-up in the surf, its fires ebbed and the creature bled to death.

Perseus unchained Andromeda and she led him to her father's palace, where Perseus claimed her for his bride. A grateful King Cepheus and Queen Cassiopeia laid on a tremendous feast and wedding celebration. Afterwards, Andromeda bade a fond farewell to her parents, Perseus swept her up in his arms and flew swiftly to his home island of Seriphos.

They arrived to find King Polydektes and his guardsmen just storming the cottage of the old fisherman, prepared to carry away Danaë by force. Perseus wasted no time in yanking out the Medusa head from the leather sack and petrifying the king and all his men. Then, briefly, Perseus left his wife and mother, and went to the forest, where again he met Athena, Hermes and Hades, and returned the gifts they had lent him. To Athena he presented the Medusa's head, and ever afterward that goddess carried it affixed to the front of her shield. You can see it thus represented on many a statue of Athena.

Now Perseus decided it was time to forgive his grandfather, King Akrisios, for his long-ago cruelty, and to make peace with the old man. So he set out for Argos. On the way he stopped at Larissa, the chief city of ancient Thessaly, where a sort of early version of the Olympic Games was in progress. Perseus dallied to enter some of the contests. When he competed at throwing the discus, he threw it farther than any champion ever had before. It whirled clear across the stadium and into the crowd of spectators, where it struck and killed an elderly gentleman. Perseus would have been chagrined in any case, but he was even more so when he learned that the victim was King Akrisios. The oracle's prediction had come true after all.

This made Perseus next in line for the throne of Argos, but in his remorse he refused to accept it. Instead, he and Andromeda went to live in Tiryns, a city near Argos, where it is said they founded the thriving culture later known to archaeologists as the Mycenaean civilization. They also founded a family, and one of their granddaughters, Alcmene, living at Thebes, gave birth to the greatest of Greek heroes.

HERAKLES

Alcmene, too, got involved with the ever-lustful Zeus just as had her grandmother, and of their union was born the all-powerful, all-conquering Herakles. However, the goddess Hera was irate at her husband Zeus' latest infidelity, and jealous of the child, so she did everything she could to make the baby's life miserable—or even to end it. While Herakles was still an infant, Hera sent two venomous snakes slithering into his cradle, but he was already so strong that he seized one in each hand and strangled them to death.

It was obvious that Herakles was destined to be a hero. From childhood he was taught by master horsemen, charioteers, wrestlers, swordsmen, lancers and archers. When barely out of his teens, he led a force of other young men from Thebes in a war against the neighboring city-state of Orchomenus, and defeated it. In gratitude, the king of Thebes gave Herakles his beautiful daughter Megara in marriage. For several years Herakles and Megara lived happily together, but Hera was still keeping a vindictive eye on Herakles, and cursed him with a fit of insanity. In that blind madness Herakles killed his beloved wife and their two children.

The madness soon passed, and Herakles was devastated by what he had done, all unknowing. He made a pilgrimage to the oracle at Delphi to ask how he could atone for his terrible deed. The oracle decreed that he must abase himself before his uncle, the cruel King Eurystheus of Tiryns, and serve him—obeying his every command, however distasteful—for twelve long years. Eurystheus, a puny and ugly man, detested his handsome, virile nephew about as much as Hera did. So each year he sent Herakles on a mission from which he hoped the hero would never return. These exploits (which have become known as the Twelve Labors of Herakles) were fraught with many adventures and perils.

First, Eurystheus sent Herakles to fetch the skin of a monster lion that was ravaging the valley of Nemea. This lion had an impregnable hide that could not be pierced by any weapon, but this did not faze Herakles. After trying in vain to kill the beast with sword, lance and arrows, he simply leaped upon it, got one iron-muscled arm around its neck and choked it to death. He had more of a problem in trying to skin an animal that couldn't be cut with metal—until he thought of using one of the dead lion's own claws. Herakles returned to Tiryns wearing the lion's pelt, with its fanged head as a helmet, and this is how he is most often represented in statues and paintings.

Historians have suggested, on the basis of this first Labor, that Herakles was a real man who actually lived in Greece at some time around 1550 b.c., who may have been a valiant hunter and who did slay a marauding lion. That feat would have been remembered and told by the storytellers over the years, with each of them embroidering Herakles' life story with more and ever more wondrous achievements.

Needless to say, Herakles coped equally heroically with the next eleven Labors. Then, a free man at last, Herakles went about business of his own. He killed a sea monster by leaping down its throat and hacking his way out from inside its stomach. He put down a rebellion of the lesser gods who sought to dethrone his father Zeus. He also married again, this time to another lovely princess named Deianira. This, however, proved to be a disastrous mistake.

Deianira sulked whenever he went off on one of his journeys and fretted that he'd meet and fall in love with someone else. Herakles, of course, never suspected her jealousy. Once a centaur named Nessos seized Deianira when she was picking flowers in a wood, and tried to carry her off. Herakles happened to be near by, and shot the half-man-half-horse with a poisoned arrow. Dying, Nessos apologized to Deianira and told her to mop up some of his spilled blood and keep it for a love charm. Should Herakles ever prove unfaithful, said the centaur, she had only to daub him with the blood to recapture his love forever.

Not long afterward, Herakles was on his way home from one of his adventures, leading a train of captured prisoners. Rumor ran before him—that one of the captives was a beauteous maiden with whom the hero was smitten. The jealous Deianira wove a sumptuous ceremonial cloak, smeared the inside of it with the centaur's charmed blood, and sent it by a messenger to Herakles on the road, that he might wear the cloak to make an impressive entrance into the town. No sooner had the messenger departed than Deianira noticed a drop of the blood had spilled on a chip of wood, and the wood was burned to ash. Horrified, she tried to recall the messenger, but too late. The cloak was presented to Herakles, and he was much pleased at this gift from his dear wife. He put it on immediately— and instantaneously regretted it. The cloak clung to him like a second skin, and began to burn like a white-hot suit of armor.

Herakles thrashed and bellowed, while the poison implacably burned away his skin, through his flesh and right into his very bones. At last, the mighty hero could hold onto the breath of life no longer. At his death, the mourning gods came down from Olympus (all but Hera) and transported him to the skies, where the constellation named for him still stands today, one star "foot" planted triumphantly on the "head" of the constellation Draco, "the dragon." Deianira committed suicide in remorse for what she had done, while, in heaven, Herakles was given for a new bride the radiant goddess of youth, Hebe. Then, said the ancients, they lived in loving happiness, with Herakles as young and strong as he had been in his prime.

JASON

During Herakles' lifetime, another Greek hero had come on the scene. His name was Jason. He grew up believing himself an orphan, but when he reached manhood his guardian revealed that Jason was really the son of the late king of Iolcos, whose throne had been usurped by one Pelias. Jason traveled to Iolcos, confronted the false king and demanded to be set in his place. King Pelias, hiding a sneer, agreed to abdicate in Jason's favor on one condition: that Jason bring him the magical Golden Fleece, the gold pelt once skinned from a winged ram and now in the keeping of the wicked King Aietes of Colchis, at the far extremity of the Black Sea. Jason vowed he'd do it.

(The legendary hunt for the Golden Fleece *is* based, rather loosely, on a true incident. It is a fancied-up telling and retelling of a Greek raiding expedition into Armenia about 1200 B.C. to seize the stores of real gold which the Armenians had laboriously washed out from their river sands—using the fleece of sheepskins to catch the gold particles.)

Jason sent heralds over all Greece to summon other heroes and would-be heroes to join the expedition, while the craftsman Argos built Greece's first warship, the *Argo*. Its prow was an oak beam enchanted by the goddess Hera so that it was capable of speech and (like modern-day radar) was able to warn the helmsman of unseen hazards ahead. When the *Argo* sailed, Jason had been joined by such stalwarts as the master musician Orpheus, the great hunter Peleus and, for ship's surgeon, the master physician Asklepios. When the *Argo* departed, Peleus' baby son waved goodbye from the arms of his nurse; the baby was named Achilles, and we shall meet him again.

Altogether, the Argonauts numbered fifty-three men and one woman, Atalanta. As the oak-beam prow guided them across the Aegean Sea, through the narrow Dardanelles and into the Sea of Marmara, the Argonauts had many encounters and adventures. Their voyage nearly ended when they came to the narrow strait called the Bosporus, which leads from the Marmara into the Black Sea.

No other ship had ever sailed through here, because the Bosporus flowed between the awful Clashing Rocks, two great stone mountains flanking the strait, which intermittently slid apart and gnashed together like a stamping press. The Argonauts raised all sail, manned all oars and—when the rocks were just opening and the oaken prow shouted "Go!"—pulled mightily to get through before the mountains crashed together again. The *Argo* barely made it, with the rocks just nipping a bit off the rudder. Having finally, for the first time, failed to crush a victim, the Clashing Rocks shuddered to a standstill, and have stayed that way ever since.

The Argonauts crossed the whole of the Black Sea and came at last to Colchis. There Jason politely asked King Aietes if he might have the gift of the Golden Fleece. Aietes, also hiding a smile, said yes, certainly—but on one condition—that Jason yoke the king's two favorite bulls, plow up a nearby field, and in the furrows sow some special seeds. At which the king handed Jason a helmet full of dragon's teeth. This seemed no great chore, so Jason agreed to plant the seeds at the next dawn. When leaving the throneroom, however, Jason was intercepted by the king's daughter, Medea, who had fallen in love with the young man at first sight. Now Medea, though beautiful and graceful, was known far and wide to be an accomplished witch. She told Jason he was in grave danger but—if he would love her in return—she would use her sorceries to keep him safe. She whispered instructions to him, and gave him magic herbs with which to anoint himself.

Jason learned his danger the next morning when the bulls were led out for him to harness. All the Argonauts were appalled. The bulls were as big as elephants, had hooves and horns of brass, and from their brass nostrils they snorted gouts of fire that singed the grass about them. Jason, coated with the juice of Medea's herbs, did not feel the fire at all, and amazed King Aietes by calmly yoking the terrible bulls to a plow and proceeding to scatter the dragon's teeth in the furrows he left behind him. As he proceeded, the dragon's teeth began to sprout—but the sprouts were iron, and as they grew they were seen to be war helmets. They grew higher, and under each helmet was a warrior, fully armed and armored. By the time Jason finished his plowing, he was surrounded by a whole army that began to converge on him.

Following Medea's instructions, Jason tossed a gleaming rock into the middle of the horde. The warriors, having been born of the earth, coveted the pretty rock and began fighting among themselves to get it. Many of them slew one another and in the commotion Jason drew his sword and killed the rest.

· Defeated and disgruntled, King Aietes was forced to show Jason the enchanted grove where, on a tree branch, hung the glowing Golden Fleece. Around the tree, however, was coiled a crested serpent, ready to kill anyone who approached. But as the minstrel Orpheus plucked on his lyre, the serpent swayed to the music, and then fell into a happy doze. Jason seized the Fleece, took Medea by the hand and before Aietes could think up some other hindrance they and the rest of the Argonauts were safe on their ship.

Back in Iolcos, Jason and his companions were received as heroes, with great festivals, rejoicing, and a splendid wedding ceremony for Jason and Medea. The Golden Fleece served as their marriage bed. Afterward, Jason delivered the Fleece to King Pelias as he had promised, but that stubborn king refused to relinquish his throne—so Medea killed him by enchantments. This pleased neither Jason nor the people of Iolcos. In all conscience, Jason could not claim the crown under such conditions. He and Medea stole away to Corinth, where they lived for ten years.

Medea was still a witch, however, and witches are notoriously hard to live with. In time, Jason lost all his love for her, and instead found himself falling in love with Corinth's Princess Glauce. Medea soon learned of this and, pretending friendship, sent to Glauce a beautifully woven robe. The moment Glauce tried it on, it clung to her and began to burn. She died while wearing it. When Jason heard of this tragedy, he rushed to Medea in a rage—only to find that she had also murdered their two children. Before he could lay hands on her, she leaped into a magical winged chariot and flew away, out of his life forever.

Jason was a destroyed man, deprived by Medea of his rightful kingdom, his children and his new love. For his few remaining years, he simply wandered along the seashore, a shambling old beachcomber scorned and despised by everyone. One day he sat down to rest in the shadow of his old ship *Argo*, now, like him, a forlorn hulk beached on the sands. While he sat there, the oaken-beam prow, rotted loose from the keel, fell and crushed him to death.

ATALANTA

The other Argonauts, long dispersed by this time, had gone about their own business, but one of them is worth following. Atalanta, the sole female among the crew, was certainly a rarity in an age when every hero was a male. At her birth, she had been rejected by her father—who had wanted a son—and was given to the tribe of centaurs to raise. They reared her to be stronger, braver, and a better warrior than most men, so she came to hold men in low regard. Atalanta was no bulgy, musclebound, lady-wrestler type, however; instead, she was gorgeous.

After her return on the *Argo*, many men paid court to her, but she set an insuperable condition. She would marry only the man who could outrun her in a footrace; if he lost he forfeited his life. Many men had tried, and lost, and died. Then, rather to her own surprise, Atalanta fell in love with a youth named Milanion. But she could not lower her standards; if he wanted her, he'd have to run against her. Fortunately, Aphrodite, the goddess of love, who never could bear to see a romance thwarted, arranged for Atalanta to lose the race—and to end up happily married to the equally happy Milanion.

ACHILLES

You will remember how another Argonaut, the hunter Peleus, as he sailed away, had waved goodbye to his infant son Achilles on the dock. That baby had been fathered by Peleus on the sea goddess Thetis, hence he was already a demigod. To make sure that he would be a hero as well, Thetis took the child, as soon as he was born, and dipped him in the underworld river Styx, which had the effect of making him invulnerable to all weapons. She held him by the heel as she did this; thus that heel was the only place where Achilles could be cut or stabbed or bruised.

Achilles grew to manhood just in time to enlist in the Greek army against Troy. Legend has it that this war was sparked when Prince Paris of Troy wooed the beautiful Queen Helen away from her husband, King Menelaus of Sparta, and took her across the sea to the high-walled city of Troy (on a hill in what is now Turkey, overlooking the Dardanelles strait). The furious Menelaus gathered troops from all over Greece, built an armada of warships and sent them to wipe Troy off the map. The lovely Helen has been referred to ever since as "the face that launched a thousand ships." (This legend is only a legend. We know there *was* a Greek-Trojan War about 1250 B.C., but the Greeks were more likely battling for control of the Dardanelles and for control of the shipping trade along that sea route.)

On the Greek side, leading thousands of troops, were Agamemnon (the commander-in-chief), Achilles, Diomedes, Odysseus, the giant Ajax, and numerous other soon-to-be heroes. Leading the defense of the city of Troy were its King Priam, his two mortal sons, Paris and Hector, and his demigod son Aieneias (born of Aphrodite). Even the gods took sides. Aphrodite, naturally, was for Troy, as were Ares, god of war, and Iris, goddess of the rainbow. For Greece there were Hera, Athena and Achilles' mother Thetis. Zeus and Apollo remained basically neutral. According to Homer's *Iliad*, the war lasted for ten years, with the Greeks' patient, the siege interrupted only briefly when the Trojans would occasionally sally forth from the city walls to fight a short indecisive battle and then duck back into the city again. In the tenth year, however, the war finally reached a climax.

Achilles, who was a magnificent warrior and foremost of the Greeks, had a peppery temper and was easily insulted. Now he quarreled with his chief, Agamemnon, over a girl and, in a fury, called his own troops from the siege, retired some distance away and simply sulked in his tent. The Trojans were heartened by Achilles' disappearance from the battlefield. They poured out of the city in full strength and began to give the remaining Greeks a real trouncing, even forging as far as the seaside and burning several Greek warships.

Achilles was distressed to see the Greek army on the verge of defeat, but he was too stubborn to rejoin the fray. Instead, he suggested to his lieutenant, Patroclus, who had been his friend

since boyhood, "You put on my armor and show yourself on the battlefield. The Trojans will think I'm back in the fight, and that will be enough to frighten them into retreat."

Patroclus obeyed, but the ploy failed. Hector of Troy was not too scared to tangle with the supposed Achilles. He killed poor

Patroclus, and then stripped off the armor he was wearing. This unexpected turn of events so enraged Achilles that he forgot his grudge and decided to re-enter the battle. He cried aloud to his goddess mother Thetis; she hurried to Hephaistos, the armorer of the gods, who swiftly forged a new suit of armor for her son.

Dressed in his shining new armor, Achilles, in a horse-drawn war chariot, charged into the fray, as Homer puts it, "like a driving wind that whirls the flames this way and that way. He chased his victims with the fury of a fiend, and the earth was dark with blood. His chariot was sprayed with the blood thrown up by the horses' hooves. And Achilles pressed on in search of glory, bespattering his hands with gore." He slashed his way through the whole Trojan army in order to find and slay Hector.

Then Hector's brother Paris fired a poisoned arrow at Achilles' breast, but his aim was off and the arrow accidentally struck Achilles in the heel—the one spot where he could be wounded—and he died of the poison. The Trojans seized the body and would certainly have mutilated and disgraced it. But the usually gentle Ajax, a gigantic man, now fought like a demon to cleave his way through the Trojans to the fallen Achilles and carry his corpse back to the Greek camp.

Ajax asked that he be given the dead hero's god-forged armor, which every other Greek officer wanted, too. Agamemnon finally decreed that Ajax and Odysseus should wrestle for the prize. Odysseus, who would have been no match for the giant Ajax in a fair fight, fought foul and won, and Agamemnon awarded him Achilles' armor. At this, says the legend, Ajax went mad and committed suicide with his own sword. From his blood sprang a showy blue flower, known today as the rocket larkspur (*Delphinium ajacis*), which bears his name on the leaves in Greek letters, AI, which also means "woe."

Bereft of their hero Achilles, the Greeks fell back on a ruse. Pretending to be totally defeated, they withdrew from further combat and spent some days building a gigantic wooden horse which the watching Trojans took to be a monument to Achilles. Then they trudged down to their ships and sailed away. Surely you know what happened next. The triumphant Trojans came cheering out of their city and hauled the horse within the walls as a symbol of victory. That night, while the Trojans relaxed and drank and sang and celebrated, a secret panel in the horse's side slowly opened and there crept out the handful of warriors the Greeks had hidden inside. They, in turn, quietly opened the city gates and the Greek army, which had sailed back to land under cover of darkness, surged in and overwhelmed the city, slaughtering almost all the people and burning Troy to the ground. Among the few Trojans who escaped was Aineias, who fled to what is now Italy and allegedly found the city of Lavinium, which was to become Rome.

ODYSSEUS

The Greek leaders herded their troops back aboard the ships and, each with his separate fleet, they set sail for their separate homelands in Greece. One fleet, that of Odysseus, took fully ten years to get home to Ithaca. During those ten years, Odysseus had enough adventures to make him, too, a hero. (He had not exactly been one before. Odysseus was probably history's first draft dodger. When Menelaus and Agamemnon had started recruiting warriors to go and fight at Troy, Odysseus had pretended insanity so he wouldn't be called upon—but that didn't work. Later, he hardly behaved heroically in his wrestling match with Ajax.) But now, on his erratic homeward voyage, Odysseus encountered numerous hazards and temptations—and heroically bested them all.

At one island stop, the fleet was captured by Polyphemus, one of a race of one-eyed giants called the Cyclopes. Polyphemus imprisoned the Greeks in his cave. At each mealtime, he brained two of the men against a rock and ate them raw. Each day the giant went out with his flock of sheep, but he made a practice of always rolling against the cave entrance a boulder so huge that all the men together could not move it. One day, however, while searching the recesses of the dark cave, Odysseus found a huge tree trunk that Polyphemus occasionally used as a shepherd's staff. Laboriously he whittled one end of it down to a point, and then hid it in the gloom.

That evening when Polyphemus came home, he herded his sheep into the cave, blocked the door again, then brained and ate two men as usual. Odysseus bravely approached the giant and, presenting the monster with a goatskin full of wine, suggested a drink to wash down his dinner. Polyphemus had never tasted wine before, and soon demanded more. Odysseus thereupon handed him goatskin after goatskin, until the giant was dead drunk. He collapsed on the cave floor, the eye in the middle of his forehead closed and he began to snore. Odysseus and four men fetched the whittled tree, struggled mightily to get it upright, and positioned it over Polyphemus' head. They lifted it as high as they could, then let it drop—to plunge into that great eye! Polyphemus leaped up, roaring and rampaging, but his captives easily eluded the blind and bumbling giant. Still, they weren't free as yet, and Polyphemus swore that they'd never leave his cave, that he'd snatch them up soon or later.

Next morning Polyphemus let his sheep, one by one, out to graze, while carefully running his hand over their backs to make sure his prisoners weren't trying to escape by riding them out. The prisoners were not; they were clinging to the wool of the sheeps' bellies. Every one of them (except those Polyphemus had dined on) got away and to the ships, in which they quickly put out to sea. However, the Greeks had unknowingly offended a powerful enemy. The Cyclopes were sons of Poseidon, god of the sea, and from now on the angry Poseidon would exert every effort to prevent their getting home to Ithaca. For example, they were immediately blown off their intended course, to the land of the Laestrygonians, another race of giants, who caught and ate *all* the voyagers, except Odysseus and the crew of his flagship.

Odysseus, with his one remaining craft, next landed at Aeaea, home of the witch goddess Circe, whose favorite entertainment was turning men into animals. She proceeded to change half the crew into swine before Odysseus, praying to the gods for help, was answered by Hermes, who gave him a magic talisman for protection. When Circe discovered she had no power over Odysseus, she let his men resume their human form, acknowledged Odysseus as her master in magic—and, indeed, became such a close friend that Odysseus stayed with her (and his men with her nymphs) for a very pleasant year.

When, finally, Odysseus and his men put to sea again, their ship might have been very soon destroyed, except that Circe had warned them against some of the dangers still ahead of them. For one, they had to negotiate a narrow strait between two headlands, and skirt around the vast, sucking whirlpool called Charybdis, which had swallowed many other ships. (The strait, now called the Strait of Messina, flows between Italy and Sicily, and is still pocked with whirlpools.) In edging past Charybdis, however, Odysseus' ship had to pass close against the cliffs of Sicily, where lived the monster Scylla, a creature of twelve legs and six long necks with fanged and hungry heads. As the ship slid by, each of the six heads snaked out and plucked a man from among the crew.

Odysseus had only a few men left, and even they were lost a little later, when Poseidon sent a great storm that destroyed the ship and drowned everyone but the captain. Odysseus was cast ashore on the island of the nymph Calypso, who fell in love with him and kept him with her for several years. Odysseus was not entirely happy with this arrangement—he yearned to get home to his wife Penelope, whom he had not seen for some seventeen years. Finally, Calypso gave him materials to build a makeshift boat, and Odysseus was once again on his way.

After many more adventures and delays, Odysseus eventually— Poseidon must have been napping—made it all the way to his home island of Ithaca. He was met at the shore by the goddess Athena, who warned him to approach his castle with caution. During his absence, said Athena, Penelope had been continuously besieged by exactly one hundred and twelve suitors, who insisted Odysseus must be long dead and pestered her to choose one of them as her new husband. So far, Penelope had managed to put them off by saying she wouldn't choose until she had finished the tapestry she was weaving. And she made sure it was never finished, for each night she unraveled what she had woven during the day.

So Odysseus crept into his own castle disguised as a beggar. He might merely have shooed out the fortune-hunting men who importuned Penelope. But they greeted the beggar with insults, jeers and blows. With this, Odysseus cast off his rags and straightened up, bow and arrows in his hand. He slew every one of the hundred and twelve suitors and, for the first time in twenty years, at last, he embraced his chaste and faithful Penelope.

There have been many more heroes among the ancient Greeks and Romans. But we have met enough of them to demonstrate how they remain part of our heritage and legendry. Perseus and the sea serpent almost certainly influenced the legend of St. George and the dragon. Danaë, her brass tower and her "shower of gold" doubtless inspired the fairy tale of Rapunzel in her tower, admitting her lover by "letting down her golden hair." Medea is the prototype of every "wicked stepmother" in many another fairy tale.

And witness what these heroes and gods have added to our language. Any long and hazardous or heroic journey is called an "odyssey." A person faced with two alternatives of action, equally unpleasant, is said to be "between Scylla and Charybdis." In wartime, any infiltration of spies or commandos inside the enemy's lines is known as a "Trojan horse" maneuver. A weak point in a person's physique or character is called his "Achilles' heel." A tremendous undertaking or accomplishment is called herculean, after Hercules/ Herakles. A tall and well-built woman is described as "junoesque," after Juno/Hera. We often call hell by the name of the underworld god Hades (the word "hell" itself came from the name of the Norse underworld goddess Hel). Aphrodite, the goddess of love, gave us "aphrodisiac," meaning a love potion.

SIEGFRIED

Now come two thousand miles north of Greece, to hear a legend that is told from Germany and Scandinavia to Iceland, and to see how a single hero may exist in two far apart and different cultures —or, if you prefer, how two isolated heroes may have amazingly similar adventures.

In this case, the hero is Siegfried, who supposedly lived somewhere in the far northland in that same era of the Greek heroes. There is no evidence of commerce or other connection between Greece and northern Europe at that time, and there is no way of knowing how the Greek and Norse people may have exchanged hero stories, or whether the similarities are pure coincidence. At any rate, in Siegfried's saga you will find startling parallels to the stories of Perseus, Achilles and Atalanta. These parallels are so very obvious that I shall not even pause to point them out.

One of Siegfried's many exploits was the slaying of the terrible dragon Fafnir. When the monster serpent was dead, Siegfried bathed in its blood, and this made him invulnerable to all weapons —except in one spot. Unnoticed while he anointed himself, a leaf had drifted down from a tree and stuck to his back, so that this one spot was left unbloodied and unprotected. Siegfried also found in the dragon's lair a cap that would make him invisible whenever he put it on.

Sometime later, Siegfried came to a hill, the top of which was ringed by fire. Thanks to his bloodbath, Siegfried easily made his way through the flames—except that his back got slightly singed, which is when he discovered for the first time that he had left one spot unprotected. Atop the hill he found a beautiful Valkyrie, one of the warrior maidens of Norse legend, lying on a couch in an enchanted sleep. (Here, no doubt, we have the genesis of the Sleeping Beauty fairy tale.) Siegfried woke her with a kiss, introduced himself—her name was Brunhild—and they fell in love at first sight. Siegfried told her he had some more traveling to do, but that he would hurry back and they would be wed.

Many miles to the south, Siegfried came to the castle of King Giuki and Queen Grimhild, who recognized the already legendary young hero and gave him a warm welcome. They also recognized what a valuable ally he would be in their frequent wars, and decided to marry him to their daughter, Princess Gudrun. Now Queen Grimhild happened to be a witch, and it was easy for her to slip a love potion into Siegfried's drinking-horn that instantly made him forget his passion for Brunhild and adore Gudrun instead.

Before that, though, Siegfried had done a lot of talking and bragging about Brunhild and her charms; enough to make Gudrun's brother, Prince Gunnar, fall in love with Brunhild sight unseen. He begged Siegfried to lead him to her abode and help him win her. Siegfried, now regarding Brunhild with indifference—as merely some girl or another he had met in his wanderings—heartily agreed, and he and Gunnar rode forth together.

A considerable time had passed by now. Brunhild had understandably concluded that Siegfried had forgotten her, so she had come to hold all "fickle men" in low regard. She declared bitterly that she would marry only a man who could best her in a contest of strength and agility. The test was this: she would throw a heavy boulder as far as she could, and then, from where she stood, leap past that boulder. Any would-be husband must throw the boulder farther, and leap farther, or forfeit his life. During Siegfried's long absence, many a suitor tried and failed, and died.

Now came Siegfried and the love-smitten Gunnar, who heard the terms of the contest and immediately realized he was no match for this junoesque Valkyrie. Siegfried told him not to worry. He donned Fafnir's cap and, thus invisible, accompanied Gunnar to the field where Brunhild awaited. Brunhild tossed her boulder farther than ever before and then easily leaped past it. Gunnar picked up his boulder (or, rather, he and the unseen Siegfried did so) and the two of them threw it far past Brunhild's. Then Siegfried took Gunnar in his arms and, with one great leap, carried him well past the boulder. Brunhild grudgingly agreed to marry Gunnar—though she was startled, puzzled and hurt when they were joined by Siegfried (who was now visible) and he coolly congratulated them on their betrothal.

The three rode to King Giuki's court, where a double ceremony was held for the marriage of Siegfried and Gudrun, and Gunnar and Brunhild. They all went on living there quite sociably—except for the unhappy Brunhild, who had never stopped loving Siegfried and was naturally jealous of Gudrun. Indeed, she taunted Gudrun whenever she got the chance: "Your husband Siegfried is inferior to my Gunnar. My husband is a prince, yours is merely his underling." Finally Gudrun was stung to retort; she told Brunhild that it wasn't really Gunnar but Siegfried who had bested her in that athletic contest.

Brunhild was livid with anger. She began hinting to her husband that Siegfried was a dangerous rival to have around. She convinced Gunnar that Siegfried could overthrow him at any moment and replace him as heir to the kingdom. Gunnar finally agreed that Siegfried must go, but reminded Brunhild that he was said to be unkillable. So Brunhild bribed a man named Hagen, one of Gudrun's servants, to wheedle Siegfried's fatal secret from Gudrun: that he could be stabbed in just one place.

Whereupon Gunnar invited Siegfried to go hunting, and they took Hagen along as their arms bearer. Deep in the forest, Siegfried dismounted from his horse to drink at a spring. As he leaned over the water, the treacherous Hagen plunged a spear into the one vulnerable spot on his back. Siegfried sagged, toppled and died. His body was taken back to the castle to be ceremonially burned —as was the Norse custom—on a towering funeral pyre of wood. At the sight, Brunhild forgot her jealousy and remembered her love. Weeping, she ran from the crowd of mourners and climbed onto the pyre to burn beside her Siegfried.

Some Heroes Who Might Have Been...
And Some Who Never Were

A celebrity is a person who is
famous because he is well known.
—Anonymous

In your reading, you may already have encountered Beowulf. The Beowulf epic is regarded as "the most precious relic of Old English literature," and is taught in many colleges. The story has come down to us in one single manuscript, lovingly preserved in the British Museum. It was written about A.D. 1000, but the story it tells occurred (*if* it occurred) perhaps as long ago as did Siegfried's adventures. We call the Beowulf saga "Old English" because the original manuscript was written in an archaic form of our language. But actually the story was brought to the British Isles long before the year 1000 by invading Danish Vikings who settled there. Beowulf's adventures took place in Scandinavia, but later British storytellers appropriated them and relocated them to various parts of Britain.

BEOWULF

Beowulf was already a warrior hero and a daring adventurer in his native Sweden when he received a call for help from King Hrothgar of Denmark. For twelve years, Hrothgar had been unable to occupy his royal palace, because there dwelt in the nearby deep forest a monster named Grendel, of human form but bestial behavior. When the palace was occupied, Grendel would force his way in, every night, and kill and eat one or more of the tenants. So Hrothgar, his family and his attendants had all deserted the palace. Now he begged Beowulf to make the royal residence habitable again.

Beowulf soon came with fourteen sturdy companions. Hrothgar and his retinue met them at the palace, laid on a princely feast for them, and then all but Beowulf and his men discreetly departed. The guests had no sooner settled down on their bearskin pallets to sleep, however, than Grendel came crashing through the palace portals. He seized one of Beowulf's men and bashed his head against the stone wall. Without time to put on his armor or even to arm himself, Beowulf grappled with the monster and—himself a man of great strength—succeeded in tearing off one of Grendel's arms at the shoulder. Spouting blood and howling with pain, Grendel fought loose and fled. The next morning, Beowulf and his party followed the trail of blood and found that it ended in a dismal swamp. Apparently the creature had stumbled in and drowned.

Hrothgar and his court gleefully moved back into the palace and threw a big celebration, only to have their revels interrupted by the invasion of another monster—Grendel's fearsome mother. She, too, seized and carried off one of the nobles. This time, Beowulf followed in close pursuit, sword in hand, and saw the female demon disappear into a pool in that same swamp. Beowulf dived in behind her, and found himself in a vaulted underwater chamber. There lay the body of Grendel, dead from loss of blood. And in a moment, thanks to Beowulf's sword, the body of the mother monster lay beside it.

Richly rewarded by the Danes, Beowulf led his men back to Sweden. There, King Hygelac and his son Heardred also honored their country's greatest hero with lands and titles. After the reign of Heardred, Beowulf was made king by popular demand, and ruled wisely and well for fifty years. Then the country was ravaged by a fire-breathing dragon, and the royal palace itself was burned to the ground. Though an old man by now, Beowulf armed himself and led eleven knights to the dragon's cave.

The giant serpent squirmed out of its lair, spewing fire. All the knights fled, except for a youngster named Wiglaf, and Beowulf himself was almost overcome by the flames. He and Wiglaf between them finally managed to slay the dragon, but Beowulf was mortally burned. His last words were to name Wiglaf as his successor to the throne. Beowulf's body was burned in the Viking style and his ashes were interred in a great mound on a high coastal cliff to be a landmark for other Norsemen far at sea.

There is *some* truth in this tale. Ancient Scandinavian histories do record the sea-warring deeds of two kings named Hygelac and Heardred in the sixth century, though there is no mention of the hero Beowulf in those or any other documents earlier than the Old English manuscript already cited. But his deeds were commemorated in Britain long after Beowulf was supposed to have lived. For ages, two ponds in England—one in Wiltshire, the other in Staffordshire —each bore the name "Grendel's Mere." And in Derbyshire there was a hillock called Drakelow, which is Old English for "dragon's lair."

WAYLAND THE SMITH

In that same chronicle of Beowulf is mentioned another character whom the British soon appropriated for their own. He was already known in Scandinavian legend as Völundr and in German folklore as Wieland. The English called him Wayland the Smith. His story is full of all kinds of fairy-tale fantasies, and Wayland himself is often less than heroic. Some versions describe him as King of the Elves, and have him married to the beautiful Svanhvit, or "swan maiden," who finally deserted him because she could no longer resist the urge to migrate like the swans, and so flew away. But most stories are content to call Wayland merely the most cunning smith (or artisan) of all time, capable of forging wondrous weapons and tools.

Once, while visiting the court of a certain King Nidothr, Wayland was challenged by the king's own smith, Amilias, who was envious of Wayland's reputation. They dueled, and Amilias was killed, at which King Nidothr offered Wayland the post of castle smith, and even built him the most modern and well-equipped smithy in the land. But Wayland wanted to be on his way and bound to no man. So the king employed a most practical way of making the smith stay put: he cut off Wayland's legs. Immobilized and seemingly resigned to his fate, Wayland crawled into his new workshop, promising King Nidothr he would emerge with a miraculous new invention. He did finally emerge, but only to slaughter the king's two sons and violate his daughter. And he did bring out a new invention: a pair of hand-forged wings—perhaps inspired by his one-time swan-wife—on which he soared away and was never seen again.

Much later, Wayland makes other appearances in British literature. In the legend of King Arthur, the magician Merlin is supposed to wear a sword fashioned by the fabulous smith. Wayland is mentioned in Sir Walter Scott's *Kenilworth,* and he is the prototype of the archvillain Aaron in Shakespeare's *Titus Andronicus*—even at one point snarling, "If one good deed in all my life I did, I do repent it from my very soul." But historians who have made scientific studies of folktales date the Wayland legend back to beyond history. They say he is meant to represent the coming of the Iron Age to northern Europe about five hundred years before Christ, when sharp iron swords first replaced the blunt Bronze Age weapons, and that the smith's aspects of both hero and villain represent the different uses—good and bad—to which a sword can be put.

Väinämöinen

Before we leave the far northland, however, let us meet a hero of long ago in Finland, one whose story is so *very* mythic and supernatural that we can in nowise relate it to reality. This story has existed from time beyond counting, but only in fragmentary word-of-mouth versions—each differing according to which storyteller was reciting it. It was not set down in writing until little more than a century ago—by scholars who tried to make all the fragments fit together into an understandable whole. It is a very long poem which the Finns call the *Kalevala.*

The *Kalevala* begins before the world existed. The "daughter of the atmosphere" Ilmatar had been wandering for seven hundred years in the empty wastes of space when finally she began to feel lonesome. She called to another god in the universe, one Ukko, who sent her an eagle. The eagle built a nest on Ilmatar's lap and in it laid seven eggs. Out of the substance of these eggs the visible world was then shaped.

This world was empty of people, however, until the hero Väinämöinen came (from somewhere unexplained) and found (somewhere unexplained) the exquisite lady Aino. From these two northern counterparts of Adam and Eve, the whole human race descended. But then Aino, like Wayland's swan maiden, deserted her mate and disappeared into space. So Väinämöinen began wandering the world in search of another bride.

Väinämöinen, unlike Adam, had two brothers, one of whom, Ilmarinen, was the world's first inventor. He constructed a magical mill, called Sampo, which would grind out, on command, either gold or salt (salt was nearly as treasured as gold in early days), thus making prosperous whoever might own it. The mill Sampo was stolen from Ilmarinen by the wicked people of a country called Pohjola just when Väinämöinen's bridal quest brought him to that bleak and dismal country. Väinämöinen found no wife there, but he did engage the Pohjolans in battle to recover the stolen Sampo.

In the struggle, the mill was broken and fell into the sea. This, according to the *Kalevala,* is what made the ocean salty (and also, we can surmise, inspired the much later fairy tale "Why the Sea is Salt"). One fragment of the Sampo, however, stayed afloat and washed up on the shores of Finland, which is why, says the poem, that country has ever since enjoyed "eternal felicity." The saga ends with a virgin named Mariatta giving birth to a king who grew up to drive Väinämöinen out of the country—and what became of the hero after that, we don't know. But his eviction is supposed to represent the coming of Christianity to the northland and its conquest of the pagan religions there.

The *Kalevala* has been translated from the Finnish into several other languages. Only scholars read it these days, but—it may surprise you to know—*you* have encountered one aspect of the *Kalevala.* Surely you are familiar with the poem *Hiawatha* by Henry Wadsworth Longfellow and its peculiar rocking-horse rhythm:

> By the shores of Gitche Gumee,
> By the shining Big-Sea-Water . . .

When he wrote that, the American poet Longfellow borrowed not the story of the *Kalevala* but its meter and scansion (eight-syllable trochaic verse) to set down his epic of a Red Indian hero far removed in both time and distance from the mythical Finn Väinämöinen.

SAMSON

A hero almost as misty and mystifying as Väinämöinen—although in a different way—is to be found in the world's best-selling book, the *Holy Bible.* We all know of Samson, whose story is told in the Old Testament's book of Judges, but biblical scholars have never been able to explain, to their own satisfaction, just *why* Samson plays such a prominent part in that book. There is nothing "religious" about Samson's activities. He was an Israelite, and the Israelites were being persecuted by the Philistines at the time, but Samson did nothing to free his people from that harassment; indeed, he even married a Philistine. The Israelites worshipped Jehovah, but Samson was inclined to indulge his own passions and go his own carefree, reckless way, rather than follow the strict commandments of Jehovah.

But it is possible to deduce some things about Samson. Almost every known culture in the world has, at one time or another, worshipped the sun. The Israelites' distant ancestors were no exception —and the name Samson is derived from the Hebrew *shemesh,* "sun." His famous long hair may be representative of the sun's rays. It is probable that Samson was a legendary "hero of the sun" long before the Israelites of biblical times came to worship Jehovah. It is equally likely that Samson was such a popular hero that the scribes who compiled the book of Judges felt they had to include him for "reader interest," much as a modern newspaper editor will include comic strips to entice more readers.

Samson's adventures have points of resemblance to those of the Greek Herakles. For instance, when he fell in love with a Philistine woman (much to his parents' anguish) and went to fetch her to be his wife, he met a lion on the way and casually tore it apart with his bare hands. Samson got along pretty well with most of the Philistines (much to the Israelites' displeasure), but he didn't hit it off too well with his wife. She treacherously caused him to lose a bet he'd made with some of his Philistine friends, so, instead of paying off the bet, Samson slew thirty of the Philistines and abandoned his wife.

When he took a notion to come back to her, he found that she hadn't missed him at all, but had married somebody else. This so vexed Samson that he trapped three hundred foxes, tied them together, two by two, with a burning torch fixed between each pair. Then he drove these incendiary teams into the fields of the Philistines, burning up their grain, vineyards and olive orchards. Samson prudently fled to the hills after that episode, but his own people— threatened by the Philistines—handed him over to the Philistines for punishment. Instead, Samson did the punishing. With nothing but a donkey's jawbone he found lying on the ground, he brained fully one thousand of the Philistines.

By now, the Philistines were determined to do away with this pernicious giant by hook or by crook. They knew of his weakness for pretty women, so they bribed his current favorite, Delilah, to discover the source of his phenomenal strength and to let them know how he might be subdued. After telling Delilah several false stories, Samson finally confided that his strength was imparted by his long hair, which had never been cut since his birth. At which Delilah lulled him to sleep and called in a barber to shear his hair. Behind the barber came the Philistine warriors, who now had no trouble in overpowering the enfeebled hero. They put out his eyes, to make him even more helpless, and marched him in chains to the city of Gaza and threw him into prison.

When it came time for the Philistines' annual celebration in honor of their god Dagon, all the three thousand inhabitants of Gaza gathered in the local temple for the feasting, music, dancing and revelry. Samson was dragged out of his prison cell to be exhibited like a captured zoo animal. He was chained between two stone pillars of the temple, where passing Philistines could jeer and spit at him. But none of them noticed that his hair had grown back during his confinement, nor did they realize what that meant. At the height of the festivities, the sightless Samson asked a little boy standing nearby to help him brace his hands against the pillars on either side of him. The boy did, and then went away. Samson bulged his muscles "and he bowed himself with all his might; and the house fell upon the lords, and upon all the people that were therein. So the dead which he slew at his death were more than they which he slew in his life."

Cu-Chullain

We move now into historical times, our own Christian era, but we are still dealing with misty legendary heroes whom we cannot prove to have really existed. One such was Cu-Chullain, who allegedly lived sometime in the first century A.D. and was among the earliest and greatest of the heroes of Ireland. His name was originally Setanta. But when still a child he passed the workshop of a smith named Cullan and was attacked by the watchdog. Even as a boy Setanta was already strong enough to rend the hound to pieces. He was immediately sorry for the deed and told Cullan, "I shall henceforth be your watchdog, sir." So he was ever after known as Cu-Chullain, "the hound of Cullan."

He was a nephew of King Conor of Ulster and, when Cu-Chullain's parents died, Conor took him into his court as a foster son, and began training the sturdy youth as a warrior. Several other likely youngsters were training at the same time, and one of them, Ferdiad, became Cu-Chullain's dearest comrade. They progressed together through the ranks, from page to squire to full-fledged knight, and later fought side by side in many a battle for King Conor.

Cu-Chullain is unique among warrior heroes in that into every fray he took along a runty little squire named Laeg, whose only job was to make fun of his master. Whenever Laeg noticed Cu-Chullain tiring in the fight or getting careless, or relaxing his defense, Laeg would shout taunts and abuse at his master—thus angering Cu-Chullain into fighting more fiercely. With the aid of Laeg's needling, Cu-Chullain performed many feats of arms. For example, he several times repulsed the Norsemen who tried to invade the northern part of Ireland. But his most renowned battle was against the forces of Queen Maeve, the most villainous woman in Irish history.

Maeve had been first married to Cu-Chullain's foster father, King Conor. But Conor could not put up with her wicked ways, and divorced her. When Maeve left the court, she took along a few warriors still faithful to her, among them Cu-Chullain's friend Ferdiad. She next married the King of Connaught and when he died—some say of poison she slipped into his cup—Maeve became sole ruler of that province of Ireland. Next she married Ailill, King of Leinster. Between them, and counting their allies, Maeve and Ailill then controlled three fifths of the entire country.

Their marriage, however, was not so much a love match as a jealous competition. One time, just to calculate which of them was the richer, Maeve and Ailill sat down and added up their separate possessions. It turned out that they were exactly equal in worldly wealth—except that Ailill owned, among his vast cattle herds, one prize bull to which Maeve had no equal. This the greedy Maeve could not abide. She knew that back in Ulster there existed the greatest stud bull in all of Ireland, the celebrated Brown Bull of Cuailgne, and she determined to own him. She mustered her troops and sent them on a full-scale invasion of her first husband's province.

Ulster was massively outnumbered by the combined forces of Leinster, Connaught and their allies. But Cu-Chullain led the defense. With his own sword he cut down hundreds of the enemy, and his inspiration made every one of his own men fight like a dozen. Maeve's warriors were so dismayed at the losses they were suffering that they called for a truce, and proposed that the battle should decided by a one-to-one combat between champions chosen from each side. Naturally Cu-Chullain stepped forward to fight for Ulster—but his heart sank when the enemy champion came forward: his lifelong friend Ferdiad.

The two had to fight, however, and they fought hard, each wielding his sword and dagger, but they fought weeping. The combat went on from dawn to dark each day for full four days, and whenever one of them suffered a severe wound, the other would help doctor and bandage it. They both knew it had to be a fight to the finish, but neither wanted to cause the death of the other. Cu-Chullain might even have dropped his defense and let Ferdiad skewer him, but for Laeg's constant shouted insults: "You fight like a kitten, master! You fight like an old woman!" Finally, Cu-Chullain dealt Ferdiad a killing blow. As his friend fell, Cu-Chullain collapsed across his body in sheer exhaustion, but Laeg quickly propped him to his feet again, lest the enemy think the duel had ended in a draw.

Cu-Chullain lived to fight many another battle for King Conor. In his last one, he even held off the enemy after he was dead. As an old Irish chronicle tells it: "Cu-Chullain died as a hero should— on a battlefield, with his back to a rock and his face to the foe, buckler on arm and his *gae-buaid* [spear of victory] in hand." In death, he still held onto his spear, and the rock supported his standing corpse. For many days the enemy dared not attack again, until at last "they saw the vultures alight upon him."

St. George

Cu-Chullain was one of Ireland's earliest heroes because, legend or not, he was Irish and all his heroic deeds were done in Ireland, presumably for the good of Ireland. By contrast, one of England's earliest heroes was not English, never did a thing *for* England, nor did he, so far as we can prove, ever set foot on English soil. All we know is that about the year A.D. 300, the Roman Emperor Diocletian found that his empire was crumbling and blamed it on Christianity, because more and more of his subjects were becoming converted to that religion. So Diocletian outlawed Christianity, and anyone discovered practicing it was persecuted, perhaps tortured and even executed. In the year 303, a high-ranking Roman legion officer named Georgius, serving in the colony of Palestine, was discovered to be a "secret Christian" and was beheaded as a traitor to his emperor.

Some two hundred years later, when Christianity had become well-entrenched, that early martyr was canonized for having died for his religion, and named St. George. From then on, all sorts of legends began to be woven about him. It was said that instead of having meekly succumbed to his execution, Georgius had boldly spoken out for Christianity and against Diocletian, that he had distributed his money and belongings among the needy poor, that he had freed his own slaves, and that he had set out upon knightly travels and done great deeds along the way.

By the tenth century, when an Italian named Jacobus de Voragine wrote the lives of the saints, he had George traveling to Libya and finding a comely princess about to be eaten by a dragon. There's no need to repeat the circumstances, as they are identical to, and obviously pilfered from, the story of Perseus and Andromeda. Of course, like Perseus, George slew the dragon. De Voragine also suggested that George's travels had taken him over all Europe and even briefly to Britain.

There are no proofs that St. George ever did anything but get himself beheaded in a far outpost of the Roman Empire. But, nevertheless, on the slender evidence of tales told about him centuries later, St. George was acclaimed as the patron saint of England, Portugal and of the province of Aragon in Spain. The "flag of St. George," a red cross on a white field, is still the official flag of the Church of England and of the Episcopal Church in America. Also, it is incorporated into the Union Jack, the flag of the United Kingdom of Great Britain.

KING ARTHUR

Equally legendary is the story of a later English hero, probably the foremost hero of the entire English-speaking world—King Arthur, that mysterious and glittering figure who, for centuries, has tantalized the imagination of minstrels, poets, storytellers, artists, fiction writers and sober historians. So much has been written about King Arthur and his Knights of the Round Table that everyone is surely acquainted with many of that gallant band's adventures. T. H. White's magnificent and moving *The Once and Future King* is by far the best modern retelling of the legend, a book as full of wit and wisdom as it is of deeds of derring-do. We will here give only a brief account of King Arthur's story (or one of them; there are countless versions).

When Arthur was born, his father, King Uther Pendragon, gave him to the old magician Merlin to raise in secret, and to train to be the best king there ever was. Upon Uther's death, all the lords and nobles of England claimed the throne, but Merlin arranged a test. On Christmas morning, there was found in front of St. Paul's Church a great stone in which was imbedded an iron anvil and, thrust through both anvil and stone, a sword engraved in gold: "Whoso pulleth out this sword of this stone and anvil is rightwise king born of all England." The nobles each had a try, and failed, but when young Arthur attempted it he drew the sword as easily as if it had been merely in a scabbard. He was thereupon acclaimed king, set up his court at Camelot, and proved to be a wise ruler and a mighty warrior.

King Arthur married a princess named Guinevere and as part of her dowry she brought to Camelot the famous Round Table. It had seats for one hundred and fifty knights and because it was round no knight was set "above" another. At the founding of the Order of the Round Table, Arthur seated one hundred and twenty-eight knights from all England. Every year a feast was held, and any new knight who had done deeds enough to merit the honor was allotted one of the vacant seats at the table. The Order included such unforgettable heroes as Lancelot, Tristan, Bedivere, Percival, Galahad and many others well known in the Arthurian legend.

King Arthur and his knights, together or separately, had many adventures. They were dedicated to bringing Christianity to the many small kingdoms that then comprised the island of Britain. So, in one battle after another, they conquered the heathen Picts and Scots of the north (tribes of hairy, uncouth savages) and the Celts of the west, until Arthur ruled over Scotland, Cornwall and Wales as well as England. He also made allies of the unruly kings of Ireland. Even the peoples he conquered found their lot much improved. To quote from an old account: "To all who would submit and amend their evil ways, Arthur showed kindness; but those who persisted in oppression and wrong he removed, putting in their places others who would deal justly with the people. He cut roads through the thickets of the land, that no longer wild beasts and fierce men should lurk in their gloom, to the harm of the weak and defenseless. Thus, soon the peasant plowed his fields in safety, and where had been wastes, men dwelt again in peace and prosperity."

"It is all true, or it ought to be," wrote Winston Churchill, a more recent English hero. And quite possibly some of the Arthurian legend is true. But we tend to identify the Knights of the Round Table with those romantic knights of the Age of Chivalry in the twelfth and thirteenth centuries, clad in full steel armor and plumed helmets, forever riding on heroic quests, slaying dragons, rescuing maidens, jousting against each other. If Arthur and his knights lived at all, it was eight or nine hundred years earlier than this, and in a far less glamorous and far more primitive time.

Britain was occupied by Roman legions from before the birth of Christ until the early fifth century. It was toward the end of their occupation that the Romans brought Christianity to the island and converted most of the native Celts. Then the Roman Empire began to disintegrate, and the legions were gradually withdrawn to defend Rome itself. As the legions departed, Britain was invaded by the Saxons, heathens from northern Europe who worshipped the warlike Teutonic gods. The native Britons, by now a mixture of Celtic and Roman blood, had become so accustomed to the protection of the professional legionaries over the past five hundred years that they were helpless against the Saxon invasion.

One brave man *could* have arisen from the mass of frightened Britons, gathered other brave men about him, and fought to stem the incoming heathen tide. He may not even have been a native; he might have been one of the last commanders sent out from Rome. We know that the Saxons were all foot soldiers and wore no armor but bearskins. The Roman legions, however, had been composed of horse soldiers who wore armor of chain mail and heavy leather. Whether Arthur was Roman or Briton, he would have known the advantages of the Roman weaponry, armor, mounted mobility, and cavalry tactics. He could well have roamed the country with his hand-picked band of mounted "knights," recruited other brave Britons wherever the Saxons were penetrating, and won repeated victories over the ill-equipped invaders.

This conjecture is supported by the earliest chronicles we have. For instance, the Britons and Saxons appear to have fought the battle of Mount Badon about the year 516. According to the historian Nennius, there "fell nine hundred and sixty men in one day at a single onset of Arthur; and no one overthrew them but he alone." (This is unlikely. Even if Arthur had fought unceasingly during the whole twenty-four hours of that "one day," he'd have had to kill one Saxon every ninety seconds to have totaled nine hundred and sixty. No doubt Nennius meant "Arthur and his followers.")

Anyway, this supposedly real Arthur was doomed eventually to failure. He fought long and hard to preserve Britain's Christianity and civilization against the paganism and barbarity of the Saxon invaders. But the invaders were simply too many. Arthur's name fades from those ancient chronicles, while the Saxons gradually overwhelm all opposition, take over Britain, settle down and intermarry with the natives. Britain was fragmented into a multitude of little kingdoms under petty kinglets forever warring with each other. The people forgot their civilized ways and reverted to ignorance and brutishness. There descended on Britain a Dark Age that was to last for five hundred years.

We get all the romantic trappings of the Arthurian legend—the Round Table; Arthur's miraculous sword Excalibur; the countless heroic antics of the numerous different knights; the tragic love affair between Guinevere and Lancelot; the miracles performed by Merlin; the tragic romance of Lancelot and the Lily Maid of Astolat; the several knights' pursuit of the Holy Grail, and the pure and innocent Sir Galahad's brief possession of it; along with many other adventures—mainly from Sir Thomas Malory, who wrote, about 1470, *The Book of King Arthur and His Noble Knights of the Round Table*.

Malory got his material from all sorts of poems, ballads and prose romances by other authors, French and German as well as English. These works dealt generally with those glamorous knights, princesses in peril, dragons, ogres, good and evil sorcerers, of the Age of Chivalry. In short, they were fairy tales. But Malory lumped them together and wove them for all time into the fabric of the Arthurian legend.

Others continued to add to that legend. When, some while after Malory's death, his book was first printed—under the title of *Morte d'Arthur*—the publisher identified Camelot as a city in Wales. Later writers speculated that Camelot was either Caerleon in Monmouthshire or Camelford in Cornwall or Winchester in Hampshire. In fact, Malory had borrowed the name Camelot from various French tales set not even in France but in a mythical land of fancy.

Still, to this day, any of those real communities would be proud to be identified with Camelot—or even as the site of any of the Arthurian adventures. As recently as 1964, the town of Carmarthen in Wales refused to remove a traffic hazard at a street crossing—a dead, withered, propped-up old oak stump—because the wizard

Merlin was said to have been imprisoned in it by his deceitful witch-sweetheart, and is presumed to be still inside. The truth is that this particular tree, "the Priory Oak," first sprouted in the 1600's, a full eleven centuries after Merlin, Arthur and the rest supposedly lived.

But let us not be ruthless with the Arthurian legend. However much or little of it really happened, it makes a beautiful and thrilling story, well worth preserving—that there was, as Churchill wrote, "a great British warrior, who kept the light of civilization burning against all the storms that beat." Yes, it is all true . . . or it *ought* to be.

ROBIN HOOD

While King Arthur has for ages been the greatest *noble* hero of the English-speaking peoples, the greatest *commoner* hero has been Robin Hood, who is supposed to have lived sometime between 1100 and 1200. He was first mentioned (as "Robyn Hood") in a poem of the year 1377, but his legend really began to grow in popularity toward the close of the Middle Ages, in the fifteenth and sixteenth centuries.

Small wonder. At that time, the common people of Europe were downtrodden, abused, overworked and overtaxed by both their feudal lords and the high officials of the Church. The common man had to labor unceasingly to satisfy the demands of his overlord and his priest; he seldom had enough to eat; he had not the smallest freedom to do as he liked. It was only natural that he should envy and glorify another commoner—one who robbed the rich and gave to the poor, one who ate well by poaching from the king's own royal game preserves, one who was a devout Christian but hated and preyed on monks and abbots, one who defied sheriffs and tax gatherers, one who enjoyed a free and happy life in the boundless greenwood. Such a one was this Robin Hood.

He is another hero about whom too much has been written to repeat here. In brief, Robin Hood was allegedly a Nottinghamshire yeoman (an independent farmer, serf to no lord) who was unfairly cheated out of his land, and so turned outlaw. He made his headquarters in Sherwood Forest and was joined by other brave and carefree spirits who shared his grudge against those privileged few who lived richly on the labors and miseries of the many. Some stories claim that Robin's band eventually numbered one hundred and forty men. We are all familiar with the more notable members:

Little John, Robin's chief lieutenant; Will Scarlet; Friar Tuck, that most irreverent monk; Allan-a-dale; Much, the miller's son; Gilbert of the White Hand, and others.

Just as Arthur may have been a diehard Briton holding out against the invading Saxons, so Robin Hood has been represented as the last Anglo-Saxon still fighting the Normans who had recently conquered England. He detested all the officials the Normans had appointed to govern their subjects, and made life miserable for them—in particular for the High Sheriff of Nottingham and the greedy abbot of that parish.

Did Robin Hood ever really exist? Probably not. Sherwood Forest in those old days was, however, a favorite hideout for outlaws and men on the run. One of them, Fulk Fitz Warin, did rescue a comely widow, Matilda Walter, who was being pestered by the unwelcome attentions of the woman-chasing King John. Fitz Warin accomplished this by marrying the lady and taking her with him to hide out in the forest. No verifiable deed of any more daring has been credited to the numerous real Sherwood Forest fugitives. Doubtless they robbed the rich, but the only poor folk they ever benefited probably were themselves.

Robin Hood appears to have been blended from those outlaws and from a number of legends dating from both before and after the age in which he supposedly lived. Long before Robin's era, the superstitious commonfolk had believed in fairies, elves, goblins and other "little people"—among them a likable but mischievous sprite they called Puck or Robin Goodfellow. Many of the pranks that Robin Hood played on the sheriff and the abbot we can find in earlier folklore, in the capers of this Robin Goodfellow.

A much later addition to the legend was Robin's fair young lady, Maid Marian. In the 1500's, one of the few enjoyments of the English commonfolk was the occasional village festival, at which one feature was always the "morris dance." This was originally performed by five men and a boy dressed as a girl, called "Maid Marian" and evidently supposed to represent the spirit of spring. As time went by, other characters of folklore were added to the dance: Hob-Nob (or "hobby horse"), Dick-Fool, Jack-Pudding and, eventually and inevitably, Robin Hood, Friar Tuck and others of that band. Before long, Robin Hood and Maid Marian were paired off to dance together—and from there Maid Marian filtered into the Robin Hood legend as his own true love.

Some historians have tried to verify the existence of a real Robin

Hood by linking him with a man named Ranulf de Blundevill, who did live at the close of the twelfth century, and who certainly did have an adventurous life. That would make Robin no yeoman, but a noble, however, for Ranulf was the Earl of Lincoln. He fought for King John against the rebellious Welsh, he helped King John hold his throne when the barons were trying to unseat him, he went on a Crusade to the Holy Land and helped capture the city of Damietta from the infidels. He died peaceably in his bed, aged about sixty.

By contrast, Robin Hood bore no love or loyalty toward King John (because that monarch was descended from the Normans who had conquered England). He never ventured outside England, and seldom outside of Nottinghamshire. He did not die peaceably, but by the treachery of a prioress to whom he had gone when he was ailing. She, pretending to bleed him moderately—a favorite "cure" of the Middle Ages—let him bleed to death. Robin's last, feeble act was to fire an arrow through the priory window, and where that arrow struck the ground, his weeping comrades buried Robin Hood.

The Little-Known Heroes...
and the Long Forgotten

And some there be, which have no memorial;
who are perished, as though they had never been.
—Ecclesiasticus

Many a hero has never been heard of outside the comparatively small circle of people in one single nation, culture, or community that first dubbed him "hero." Many another hero has just gradually drifted out of popularity and into oblivion, usually because his deeds, while heroic, were not dramatic enough to make a story sufficiently enthralling to be repeated over and over again. Let us here unearth, from various periods of history and various parts of the world, a few of these who are little known and/or long forgotten.

GILGAMESH

The story of Gilgamesh is familiar today only to a handful of scholars. Time was, however, when Gilgamesh was the pre-eminent hero of several million people. And his adventures were certainly dramatic enough to be pilfered and, as we shall see, incorporated into the legends of many later heroes. But Gilgamesh himself has been all but forgotten, for the simple reason that the whole civil-

53

ization which revered him has itself long ago vanished. That civilization was ancient Babylonia, and we do have evidence that a Babylonian named Gilgamesh actually lived, though there is no knowing exactly when. Babylonia was, for many centuries, the most powerful empire of the Middle East, but finally weakened, disintegrated and about five hundred years before Christ was absorbed into the growing Persian Empire. All we know of Babylonia today is what the archaeologists have been able to deduce from fragmentary ruins and records.

Among the records found by archaeologists digging in the ruins of the Assyrian city of Nineveh was a series of twelve clay tablets —such tablets were all the Babylonians had in the way of books— bearing, in the Babylonian cuneiform (wedge-shaped) letters, the epic of Gilgamesh. None of these tablets has been found intact; they were all in shards; but numerous pieces were identical, proving that the Gilgamesh saga was so popular that it was copied and recopied many times. The oldest of these clay fragments dates from about the year 2000 B.C., so Gilgamesh lived *sometime* earlier—whether years or decades or centuries, no one knows.

It is certain, however, that he lived and that his legend was set down well before the Old Testament was written and before the Greek storytellers had begun to celebrate the "great ancient" heroes you met in an earlier chapter. No doubt, as has happened with every other hero of antiquity, Gilgamesh's real exploits were exaggerated and added to by the Babylonian scribes. Still, you will notice that many of his adventures long antedate (and were copied into) the legends of such heroes as Samson and Herakles, and there are many other coincidences in the course of his story.

According to the first cuneiform tablet, Gilgamesh was already a veteran of many heroic adventures when he became ruler of the city named Erech. His first act as ruler was to draft all the able-bodied citizens to build a massive defensive wall around the city. The people of Erech didn't like this enforced labor, so they determined to seek out another and sturdier hero who would dethrone Gilgamesh. It happened that in the wilderness beyond the city lived a man named Enkidu ("a strong, wild man, living with the gazelles and the beasts of the field"). The citizens of Erech sent a lovely young maiden to tempt Enkidu away from his free and idyllic life among the animals, to coerce him into "civilized" city life, and eventually to persuade him to overthrow Gilgamesh. (This episode, say many scholars, is the real source of the biblical story of Adam's being tempted by Eve.)

Enkidu came reluctantly to the city but, at their first meeting, he and Gilgamesh immediately became firm friends. The two of them made many travels and had many adventures together. For one example, they were bidden by the Babylonian sun god Shamash to seek out and destroy a formidable monster called Khumbaba, which lived in the midst of a vast cedar forest. (You will notice that the sun god's name is a mere variant of the Hebrew word for the sun, *shemesh*, from which Samson's name also derived.)

Gilgamesh and Enkidu prayed for the aid of Ishtar, the goddess of love, in this project—and with her personal help slew the monster. As payment for her services, Ishtar then demanded the love of Gilgamesh, but he spurned her, which was unwise. The scorned and angry goddess took revenge by smiting Enkidu with an illness which, from the clay tablets' description, was awful and agonizing, but unidentifiable. Anyway, it killed Enkidu, and that loss just about broke Gilgamesh's heart. (This is all reminiscent of the long friendship of Achilles and Patroclus, and Achilles' sorrow at his friend's death.)

Now Gilgamesh became obsessed with the fear of dying himself—which certainly makes him unique among all the stoic and fearless heroes we have met thus far. He set out wandering the earth, seeking some secret that would make him immortal—and he wandered for years, having numerous adventures along the way. (This wandering may have inspired the long and eventful journey of Odysseus.) At one point, finding a mountain pass guarded by a giant and a ferocious lion, he had to kill the lion and overcome the giant in order to get through. At another mountain, Gilgamesh was set upon by what the tablets call "scorpion men"—a curt description, but enough to make us visualize horrible beings. Gilgamesh did not kill these creatures, but "subdued" them and enlisted their help in furthering his journey toward immortality. The scorpion men directed him to the ferryman who plied the "waters of death." The ferryman took Gilgamesh to the farther shore, where he finally met a man who was truly immortal. This venerable fellow, named Ut-Napishtim, had lived a long and lively life and, like many old men, was only too eager to tell his story in every last detail.

Ut-Napishtim was a favorite of the gods—he said so himself, but he never said why—and thus was enabled to dodge death and disasters that demolished other men. For example, said Ut-Napishtim,

the gods had given him advance warning of a flood that was to inundate the world and drown all the wicked people in it. (This, remember, was written long before the biblical story of Noah and the flood.) So Ut-Napishtim built a tremendous boat and shepherded into it, as did Noah, a pair of every kind of animal that existed. Unlike Noah, Ut-Napishtim also took aboard numerous man-made objects like tools and weapons, *and* one of every kind of craftsman he could find—so that mankind's arts and crafts should not be forgotten, and civilization could begin again after the flood was over.

Ut-Napishtim was also the first to bury a "time capsule" (of the sort that, in our modern times, is often buried at world's fairs and such events, to be dug up centuries later and shown to future generations as picturing what our present life is like). Before the threatened rains came, Ut-Napishtim wrote out and buried an account of "the beginning, middle and end of all things." Unless Ut-Napishtim later disinterred that clay-tablet account, it still lies waiting in what is now Iraq: a buried treasure for some lucky archaeologist to find. After the flood had come, and washed the earth clean of other people, and subsided, Ut-Napishtim's ark came to rest—like Noah's—on a mountaintop, and he and his passengers set about rebuilding civilization.

Gilgamesh sat patiently through all the old man's prattling, then told him what he'd come for: the secret of immortality. Evidently grateful to have had such a willing audience, Ut-Napishtim described to Gilgamesh a magical herb that would confer on him life everlasting, and told him where to find the only specimen that grew. Gilgamesh immediately said goodbye, hurried to that place, plucked the herb—and took his eyes off it just long enough for a snake to come along and eat it. (Could this be the same serpent that cut short Adam and Eve's stay in Eden?)

All his hopes dashed, Gilgamesh wandered forlornly on his way— and suddenly encountered the ghost of his comrade Enkidu. The ghost looked none too happy with its condition, and gave Gilgamesh a woeful lecture. There was nothing pleasurable, like a heaven, for the dead to look forward to, Enkidu confided, and not even the questionable excitements of a hell. There was simply nothing at all. Nothing to do, nothing to hope or wait for, no way to communicate with the living or even the other dead, nothing but to half-exist, like a shadow, forever and ever and ever. The only faint relief the dead could know, said Enkidu, was to have their descendants remember them kindly and venerate their memory. With that, Enkidu's ghost vanished, and the twelfth clay tablet ends. We have no idea what became of Gilgamesh after that encounter. But we can guess that with his long-standing fear of death and his knowledge of what death would mean, his remaining lifetime must have been a wretched torment.

It is no accident that the Gilgamesh story was divided among *twelve* tablets. The Babylonians were the inventors of astrology, and those twelve tablets represented the twelve signs of the zodiac. Even without the written tablets in hand, a storyteller could recount Gilgamesh's adventures by using the twelve zodiacal constellations to jog his memory. The sign of Scorpio, for instance, would remind him of Gilgamesh's encounter with the scorpion men. This is why so many of Gilgamesh's adventures were woven into the legends of the heroes of other and later cultures. The Babylonian "science" of astrology was embraced by many other civilizations—Israel, Greece and Rome among them—and where astrology went, the epic of Gilgamesh went.

CHU-KO LIANG

While we have seen much borrowing back and forth of heroes and their exploits among the countries of the West, not many heroes of the Far East have filtered into western legendry. So let us move some 5000 miles east of Babylonia and some 2300 years later in time, and meet the inimitable scholar-warrior Chu-ko Liang, who lived in China in the third century after Christ.

"Brain over brawn" was always the first precept of Chinese military tradition. Therefore, about the year 220, when the ruling Han dynasty found itself threatened by an uprising led by a rebel named T'sao T'sao, the Han rulers did not trust their numerous generals to put it down. They called in for counsel a man who had never swung a sword. He was Chu-ko Liang, a sage and poet whose only previous weapons had been paper, brush, ink-block and lute. He agreed to take the field with the Han generals and give them what aid he could.

Not surprisingly, the generals and other professional soldiers resented this civilian in their midst, so they put him to the test with outrageous and impossible tasks. On the eve of a riverside battle— the Han forces on one side of the stream, T'sao T'sao's on the other —a general ordered Chu-ko Liang to produce immediately an arsenal of one hundred thousand arrows for his troops. Chu-ko had no hope of procuring or making so many. What he did was to hurry far up- stream and borrow twenty boats from a fishing village. Then he padded their sides with thick straw matting. At evening, Chu-ko had the fishermen float these boats downstream in single file past the enemy's position on the far shore. In the twilight, T'sao T'sao could not see that each boat carried no one but a helmsman. He hesitated to send his own boats out to engage them, fearing an am- bush, but he also feared an assault landing. So he lined the river bank with his archers, and they poured a hail of arrows into the threatening craft. Of course, the arrows embedded themselves in the straw padding. As soon as the boats were bristling with shafts, Chu-ko Liang let them float downstream to his general's position— and delivered the hundred thousand arrows as ordered.

Chu-ko was given his own command, and proved himself a canny tactician. On one occasion, when he was holding a town with a small body of men, T'sao T'sao approached with much greater force. Chu-ko Liang set some of his men to piling sulphur, niter and other inflammable substances on the roofs of the town, while other men went to work damming a nearby river which the enemy would have to cross. When all was ready, Chu-ko and his troops withdrew and hid at some distance from the town.

T'sao T'sao and his men crossed the river, not noticing that it was now just a muddy gully. He arrived at the town, found it deserted, decided Chu-ko had retreated, and allowed his tired troops to bed down in the empty houses. No sooner was all quiet than Chu-ko Liang's concealed archers shot fire-tipped arrows into the town— and every building went off like a firecracker. T'sao T'sao and his men fled in confusion from the inferno back to the river they had crossed. Chu-ko's men fired on them from ambush, and dropped many of them. Then, when the remainder of the army was slogging across the river mud, Chu-ko's men upstream smashed the dam they had built. The backed-up water crashed down like a tidal wave and drowned practically all of T'sao T'sao's force.

Chu-ko Liang became so feared for his unexpected methods of warfare that he sometimes didn't even have to lift a hand to win a battle. One time, hearing that a huge enemy force was marching on the city where he was then staying with just a handful of men, he quickly had all his troops change from uniforms into drab civilian dress, hide all their arms and banners, and go to work sweeping the streets with brooms. He flung open all the city gates; then, himself dressed in his scholar's gown, he sat atop the city wall with his lute, chanting poetry to a couple of young boys. T'sao T'sao's horde approached, ready for battle. But when T'sao saw the normally well-prepared Chu-ko Liang lolling in such a peaceful attitude, and with no one else in sight but street sweepers, he assumed that some devastating trap had been laid. T'sao turned his whole army about and fled. It wasn't long before T'sao surrendered entirely—more out of bafflement and frustration than actual defeat—and ceased his rebellion.

KING SE-JONG

The Oriental peoples have always been readier to make a hero of a man of wit and wisdom than one of muscle and might. The country of South Korea, for example, has had many warriors to be proud of—from Admiral Yi Soon Sin, who defeated the Japanese Navy with the world's first ironclad warship in 1592, to the numerous combat heroes of the 1950–53 war against North Korea and China. But considerably more beloved is the gentle King Se-jong who, according to legend, gave Korea what neither China nor Japan has to this day: an alphabet to write its language with.

In the year 1443 the few Koreans who could write were still using the cumbersome Chinese ideograms (complex characters expressing an entire word or sometimes a whole phrase), of which a scholar had to memorize some *fifty thousand* in order to write. In that year, says the story, the wise King Se-jong decided that his nation would be more prosperous and powerful if more of his people knew how to read and write. What was needed, mused the king, was a simple alphabet which would set down the language in writing according to its spoken sounds. Se-jong worked one out—an alphabet just as functional as ours (and considerably more simple). But the king realized that he couldn't force its adoption; he would have to convince the people that this was a gift from heaven. At night he went into the palace garden with a writing brush and a pot of honey. On the leaves fallen from the plane trees he painted, with honey, the fourteen consonants and ten vowels he had invented, one to a leaf.

The next morning, Se-jong invited the royal soothsayer for a stroll in the garden. During the night, as the king had foreseen, insects had eaten away the honeyed portions of the leaves. There now lay twenty-four leaves, each leaf etched with one of the new letters. The soothsayer noticed the leaves, as the king had intended, and gathered them up.

"This is no accident," he said to the king, in a hushed voice. "The spirits are trying to tell us something." The sage took the leaves up to his tower and spent some weeks puzzling over them, until at last realization dawned. He burst into the throneroom with the breathless news: "They are an alphabet, sire! The spirits have sent us an alphabet for writing our language!"

King Se-jong, with a straight face, expressed his astonishment, pleasure and admiration at the sage's quick solution to the mystery, and ordered that the alphabet be immediately published for the use and benefit of his people. They accepted it eagerly, concludes the legend, and that was how Korea became the first nation in the world to pioneer literacy for the masses.

WILLIAM TYNDALE

Less than a hundred years later, in "civilized" Europe, another man who tried heroically to educate his fellow men died for his pains. In the fifteenth and sixteenth centuries, the only authorized Bible was the Latin translation, and this, of course, was read only by priests. The commonfolk were discouraged from learning to read the Bible—from learning to read at all, in fact. In those days the Christian Church frowned on education. It insisted on pure, unquestioned *faith,* and decreed that any attempt at *reasoning* toward the truth was hostile to that faith. The Bible was only for the priests, and their parishioners must rely on and trust in the priests' interpretation of it. Education of the masses was therefore "heresy," a deliberate attack on the foundations of Christendom.

One obscure English priest thought differently, however. William Tyndale, though only a lowly chaplain to the household of a minor noble, determined to make the Scriptures available and understandable to everybody in England by translating them from Latin into everyday English. When he had completed a translation of the New Testament, he was immediately assailed by his superiors in the Church, and his book was forbidden to be published in England.

So Tyndale journeyed to Germany, where he succeeded in getting his English New Testament printed—though very few Englishmen ever got to see a copy. England forbade importation of the book, and the Archbishop of Canterbury even went so far as to buy up all the copies he could locate in Europe—so he could burn them! Tyndale was by now in the Netherlands, busy translating the early books of the Old Testament. And now, pressured by the archbishop, King Henry VIII of England demanded that the Netherlands hand over the errant priest for trial on charges of trying to undermine the authority of the English crown.

Tyndale went into hiding. But one of his students, a young man named Henry Phillips whom he had trained to help in the translation and whom he loved almost as dearly as a son, betrayed Tyndale to the imperial officers of the Netherlands. He was imprisoned there, tried for heresy, found guilty and condemned to die. On October 6, 1536, he was strangled at the stake and his body was burned. But his work survived, and you have probably read some of it. "His translation of the Bible was so sure and happy," as one chronicler described it, that it became the basis of the later "authorized" King James Bible of 1611, still the most popular, best-loved and best-selling version of the Good Book.

GEOFFREY HUDSON

Another English hero, little heard of since his time, was Geoffrey Hudson. He was born in 1619 into an undistinguished family, but was introduced to King Charles I and became quite a favorite at court. When the English Civil War erupted in 1642, young Hudson commanded a troop of cavalry for the king, and his heroic services won him a knighthood. Charles lost the war and was beheaded, and Oliver Cromwell took over the government of England. Sir Geoffrey Hudson faithfully accompanied the widowed Queen Henrietta into exile in Paris. But there he killed a man in a duel of honor, and fleeing from France by sea, he was captured by Barbary pirates and sold as a slave. He finally escaped, returned to England—where by now the monarchy had been restored under Charles II—and lived out his life on a handsome pension.

Sir Geoffrey's adventures might seem interesting enough, but hardly remarkable compared to those of other men—except for one thing. Sir Geoffrey Hudson was one of the smallest men who ever lived. Perfectly proportioned, but tinier even than Barnum's famous "General Tom Thumb," Hudson stood less than twenty inches tall at the time he was captain of horse! When he was thirty, Hudson began to grow a bit, and was three feet nine inches tall at his death in 1682.

Denis Papin & John Fitch

Some men who might have been acclaimed as heroes, or at least as benefactors to humanity, have been cheated of that fame—and long forgotten—because of historical circumstances or because other men simply usurped the honor due them. For instance: Who invented the steamboat? Robert Fulton, you say, the man whose sidewheel steamer *Clermont* first plied New York's Hudson River in 1807. That's what we've all been taught in school. But this is completely wrong.

More than a hundred years earlier, about 1700, Denis Papin, a French inventor of many kinds of machinery, built a successful paddlewheel steamboat. But when he tried to demonstrate his vessel to the public by steaming up the River Seine, his boat was confiscated by the authorities on a complaint from the union of boatmen, who feared that a powered craft would deprive them of making their living by rowing boats. Papin died in London in 1712, in great poverty, having squandered all his money on his inventions.

In 1786, an American named John Fitch had a paddlewheel steamboat actually carrying freight on the Delaware River. Fitch dreamed of giving his countrymen easy access to the broad rivers of the West, and thus facilitate America's expansion of her frontiers. But his countrymen feared to ride his chugging, spark-spitting craft, and jeered at Fitch as an impractical visionary. In 1793, vandals maliciously destroyed his fifth boat, which was the first in history to utilize a screw propeller instead of a paddlewheel. (Screw propulsion was not to be tried again for nearly fifty years, and then, of course, it totally supplanted the inefficient paddlewheel.) In 1798, like Papin, Fitch died in utter despair and misery.

Robert Fulton's *Clermont* was in every important respect a copy of Fitch's designs. But Fulton had wealthy and influential backers, and he knew the value of publicity. He made the public believe that the *Clermont*'s success was the first in steam navigation, and so impressed the United States Government that he was given a monopoly on building the country's steamboats (what amounted to a patent on "his" invention) for the subsequent thirty years. His statue still stands in the American Hall of Fame. But who, today, has ever heard of Denis Papin or John Fitch?

Benjamin Thomson

Another man who lived in that same era might have been one of America's most noted scientific heroes, except that the country callously and foolishly rejected and evicted him. Benjamin Thomson, whom one historian has set well above even Benjamin Franklin as "the most universal genius of America," was born in Massachusetts in 1753. He was so quick in his studies that by the age of fourteen he had mastered astronomy, algebra, geometry, calculus, and could predict a solar eclipse "within four seconds of accuracy."

When he married the young widow of a British Army colonel, it was a love match but it was also a political mistake, for the American colonies were then preparing to revolt against Great Britain. Although Thomson was a major in the New Hampshire militia, he was treated with suspicion, scorned, rebuffed, because his wife had been married to a hated "lobsterback" British officer. Not able to endure the unkind cuts of his countrymen, Thomson sadly abandoned his homeland and, in 1776, sailed to England. He never fought against his native country, but, as a scientist and fellow of Britain's Royal Society, he did work on improving gunpowder, inventing better firearms and a system of signaling between ships at sea—all developments which would have been invaluable to the Americans, had they kept Thomson on their side.

England knighted him for his contribution to science, then, after the Revolution was over, lent his services to Bavaria. There, Thomson served as minister of war and head of the police. He reorganized the Bavarian army, and even organized an army of the beggars and tramps in that country. He rounded up nearly three thousand of them, housed them and put them to work in a combination factory-and-dormitory he built for them. To the surprise of skeptical social workers, the beggars (thieves, bums, pickpockets and other riffraff) not only supported themselves but also their factory turned a profit for the state. Thomson said, "To make vicious and abandoned people happy, it has generally been supposed necessary first to make them virtuous. But why not reverse this order? Why not make them happy, and then virtuous?" In 1791, Thomson was created a count of Bavaria, and it is a measure of his undying devotion to his home country that he chose for his title Count Rumford, after his wife's New Hampshire hometown (now called Concord).

After his tour of duty in Bavaria, Count Rumford returned to England, where he became one of the first fighters against pollution of the environment, turning his inventive genius to methods for lessening the smoke from factory chimneys. He was also the first scientist to prove that heat is not (as was then believed) a substance, but is molecular motion. His other scientific achievements are too numerous to list here. Benjamin Thomson, Count Rumford, died in France in 1814 without ever having laid eyes on his native America since he was hounded out nearly four decades before. Now he is barely remembered here, even by other scientists.

HARRIET TUBMAN

An American heroine who may be well known to black readers, but is only a name to most whites, if indeed they've heard of her at all, is Harriet Tubman. For ten years, however, she was not by any means a heroine to the majority of white people; in fact she was a thorn in their sides.

The date of Harriet Tubman's birth is not known for sure—she never knew it herself, for she was born a slave in Maryland, and nobody bothered about birth certificates for slaves—but it was sometime around 1820. When she was grown to womanhood, Harriet decided that though she had been born into a slave-owning society, she hadn't been born to *be* a slave. And in 1849 she escaped from her master's plantation and fled across the border into the non-slave state of Pennsylvania. Then she decided that if she could escape, so could other Negroes, and she would help them to do so. Not only did she have to sneak them out of the shoot-on-sight Southern states but she also had to buck the opposition of whites even in the supposedly "free" states of the North.

At that time, the country was already divided on the slavery issue and the Southern states were threatening to secede from the Union. In hopes of placating the South and preserving the nation, the U.S. Congress made all sorts of wishy-washy compromises. One of these was the Fugitive Slave Law of 1850, which effectually prohibited any of the non-slave Northern states, or their citizens, from giving aid or refuge to slaves escaping from the South. Instead, the fugitive blacks were to be caught and returned to their owners.

There had long been a good number of kindly whites in the Northern states who were opposed to slavery and dedicated to the freeing of any slaves they could help. The new Fugitive Slave Law was so harsh that many other white people, previously uninterested, made up their minds to disobey it. And so there came into being an escape route and chain of hideouts (usually the cellars or barns of these white "abolitionists") stretching from the South-

ern states northward through Ohio, Pennsylvania or New York, and into Canada, where there was no ban on receiving the fugitive blacks.

This secret path to freedom came to be called the Underground Railroad, because those involved in it used railroad terms as a code when referring to it. The various routes were known as "lines," the resting places and hideouts along the way became "stations," those who led the escaping slaves from one station to the next were "conductors," and the black fugitives themselves were called "freight" or "packages."

Harriet Tubman became one of the Underground Railroad's most successful conductors. She made some twenty trips deep into the South—and for a lone Negro, getting in and traveling unchallenged was about as hard as getting out. But get in and get out she always did, and altogether she brought out more than three hundred slaves. Harriet was seldom called simply "conductor." The leading abolitionists referred to her proudly as "General" Tubman, while the blacks reverently called her "Moses," for having brought them "out of bondage into the Promised Land."

A few of the slaves may have called her less respectful names behind her back, however, for Harriet Tubman could be a no-nonsense leader. On numerous occasions, some of her slave "packages" would lose their nerve at the prospect of making their way for hundreds of miles through hostile territory, North as well as South, and would try to jump the "train" and scuttle back home. On such occasions, tough "General" Tubman would haul a loaded revolver out of her voluminous skirts—and make them move on to freedom.

Then came the Civil War, and Harriet's talents for infiltrating enemy territory came in handy. She joined the Union forces which, throughout most of the war, held the more strategic ports along the coasts of South Carolina and Georgia. Ostensibly, Harriet served as a nurse and laundress, but actually she was a spy, circulating through Rebel-held plantations and gathering valuable information from the gossip of local slaves. After the war, Harriet Tubman continued to work, lecture and agitate for the betterment of her people practically to the end of her life, which came in Auburn, New York, in 1913, at the age of nearly one hundred.

Daisy Bates

Another woman, but this one white, also heroically championed the rights of black people, though these were not Negroes, and were 13,000 thousand miles from where Harriet Tubman crusaded. She was Daisy Bates, born in Ireland and brought up in England. In the 1890's she heard how the whites in Australia were mistreating the natives of that continent, and persuaded a newspaper editor to send her there to write a series of articles on the subject.

She never came home again. She traveled through the most remote Outback of Australia, living among the aborigines and studying them, a woman alone, but enduring a hardscrabble life as lonely and arduous as that of any hardy male bushranger. As Daisy got to know the natives and their way of life, she grew to like them more and more, and gradually grew to dislike her own race. Perhaps any white with a trace of conscience would have been ashamed of his race in those days. The white settlers to a man regarded the aborigines as just another native nuisance, like the kangaroo, and fit for nothing but extermination. Even shooting was too good for them—cartridges cost money—so the farmers and ranchers poisoned the aborigines' tribal wells, or pretended friendship, invited the natives to feasts, and then fed them poisoned food.

Finally and disgustedly, Daisy Bates turned her back on the whites and moved as far from their "civilization" as she could get, settling down among the remnants of aboriginal tribes at a place called Ooldea on the bleak and empty Nullarbor Plain. There she was cordially accepted by the aborigines. Indeed, they came from hundreds of miles around to meet this one white person who understood and was kind to them. Daisy learned their numerous dialects. She studied and recorded their habits, rituals and legends. She ate what they ate. She tended them when they were ill.

The one thing she balked at doing was going naked as they did. Winter and summer, rain or shine, she wore a high-necked blouse, ankle-length skirt, a big veiled hat, gloves and high-buttoned shoes. The only other difference between Daisy Bates and her adopted tribesmen was that she could write. And write she did: angry articles for English newspapers, angry letters to the white Australian authorities, an angry book, *Passing of the Aborigines.*

"In their own country, they were trespassers," she wrote. "There was no more happy wandering. Sources of food supply slowly but surely disappeared, and they were sent away to unfamiliar places, compelled to change their mode of life, to clothe themselves in the attire of strangers, to eat foods unfitted for them, to live within walls. Their age-old laws were laid aside for the laws they could not understand. A little while, and they resorted to thieving—where theft had been unknown."

Daisy damned the white man's deliberate debasement of the black: selling him mind-rotting and fatally addictive whiskey, giving him diseases never before present in Australia, buying his women, breeding a race of half-castes despised by both whites and black. She also inveighed against the white man's despoiling of the continent itself. His cutting down of the great trees to make room for his crops and pastures—with the result that the flayed land was scoured by ever-more-frequent sandstorms. His importation of foreign animals like rabbits (for food and fur) and English sparrows (to eat bothersome insects)—with the result that both rabbits and sparrows themselves multiplied into inexorable crop-devouring hordes that haven't yet been checked.

Just as most Americans do not like to be reminded of their forebears' mistreatment of the native Red Indians, nor of their own contribution to pollution and ruination of their once-beautiful environment, neither did the white Australians like to have their mistakes pointed out. So very critical of the white man was Daisy's book that even today, as then, the white Australians prefer to pretend it never existed—and the name of Daisy Bates is seldom listed among "Australian writers." There remains, however, one monument to that gallant lady. At the site of Daisy Bates' old camp at Ooldea on the Nullarbor Plain is one of the thirteen reserves now set aside—like Indian reservations in the United States—for the exclusive occupancy of Australia's few remaining aborigines.

We'll conclude this chapter with one last and little-known hero. This one, in fact, is totally *unknown*. All he left us was a short poem, and all we know of him is that he was a soldier in the British Eighth Army, which engaged in the Tunisian desert campaign against a Nazi tank force during the Second World War. We must assume that he died there, for the poem was publicly printed after the war and no one has yet come forward to claim authorship. It was found scrawled on a scrap of paper in an empty foxhole:

> Stay with me, God. The night is dark,
> The night is cold: my little spark
> Of courage dies. The night is long;
> Be with me, God, and make me strong . . .

A Few Inadvertent Heroes

> Be not afraid of greatness: some are born
> great, some achieve greatness, and
> some have greatness thrust upon them.
> —Shakespeare

We have seen how some heroes have been cheated of the fame and
honor due them, and how others—though great heroes in their day
—have been forgotten by later generations. There were still others
who became heroes unexpectedly or without intending to. Except
for the circumstances of their time, they might have lived placid
and unremarkable lives. Instead, something forced them to take a
stand, to perform a deed, to champion a cause, or merely to die
heroically for what they believed in. And they are no less heroes
because they never intended to be heroes.

Queen Boadicea

One of the earliest inadvertent heroes in history was a heroine,
Queen Boadicea. She lived in the first century A.D. in what is now
England, and was the wife of a petty tribal king named Prautagus.
That was a time when women, even queens, were accounted to be
insignificant creatures and in every way inferior to men.

The Roman legions had by then been occupying the island for more than a hundred years. Many of the numerous small British tribal "kingdoms" had succumbed to Roman rule, but others merely acknowledged the Romans as token conquerors, while keeping their own rulers and their own ways. The Romans allowed this, so long as the tribes caused no trouble, but these semi-independent tribes were looked down upon as barbarians who were too ignorant to accept Roman civilization. Among these still aloof and self-governed tribes was the Iceni. Their king, this same Prautagus, was fearful that his lands would be stormed by other barbarians after his death, so he willed his kingdom jointly to his two daughters and to the Roman Emperor. In A.D. 61 he died, comforted by the belief that the emperor would see his daughters well married to strong kings and that his kingdom would be preserved. Unfortunately, the Roman Emperor at that time was Nero, an evil and hateful man. As always happens, his officials and subjects—from high consul down to the least centurion in the legion—tended to imitate Nero's wicked ways. On the death of Prautagus, the Roman legions invaded the Iceni territory, plundering what few riches it contained, seizing the land, carrying off the people to be slaves—and doing terrible things to Prautagus' widow Boadicea and the two daughters.

When she had recovered from her ordeal, Boadicea did what no other woman of her time would have dreamed of doing: she went to war, with herself as commander-in-chief! She gathered the demoralized Iceni, organized and armed them, and set out for revenge. Boadicea coldly commanded that no prisoners were to be taken, no enemy spared or ransomed. The order was *kill!* "by sword, cross, gallows or fire." And she was not content to kill only Romans; even more she hated the British tribesmen who had willingly submitted to Roman rule.

The first target was Camulodunum (now the borough of Colchester), actually a sort of "senior citizens center" inhabited by retired Roman soldiers and the "Romanized" Britons who were servants, merchants, tradesmen, etc. Boadicea's barbarian horde could hardly be repulsed by a town of clerkish civilians and old soldiers. Camulodunum was burned to ashes, and everyone in it, Romans and Britons alike, was massacred. That rather easy conquest impressed the other barbarian tribes still uncommitted to Roman rule, and they flocked from all over Britain to join Boadicea's standard. She found herself in command of an army of 80,000 men. The Roman legions were, of course, better armed and armored

—and had horses, which the Britons didn't—but they numbered only about 20,000 men and were widely scattered over the island.

In one engagement, Boadicea's army slaughtered every last infantryman of the Romans' Ninth Legion; only the mounted cavalrymen escaped. Then Boadicea marched on Londinium. (This siege, recounted by the Roman historian Tacitus, is the first mention ever of the town which was to become London.) The Ninth Legion had been assigned to protect Londinium, but what was left of it was galloping toward Wales to call in the reinforcement of the Fourteenth and Twentieth Legions. So the defenseless Londoners—mostly peaceable Roman traders and their British associates, dependents and slaves—fell before Boadicea's swords and torches: every man, woman and child. Next it was the turn of Verulamium (now St. Albans), likewise obliterated. In the three cities of Camulodunum, Londinium and Verulamium, Boadicea's barbarians had slain a total of 70,000 Romans along with their British allies.

But then the Roman legate C. Suetonius Paulinus, having made a forced march from Wales, arrived with his Fourteenth and Twentieth Legions, plus the remnants of the Ninth, and confronted Boadicea's tatterdemalion army on the open plain. Boadicea's original 80,000 men had been scarcely diminished; Suetonius had only some 10,000 in his legions. The day was, according to a chronicler, "bloody and decisive; on both sides it was all for all." The Romans were tremendously outnumbered, but they had better weapons, better discipline and greater tactical skill. The Romans lost many men, but they won the day. Boadicea did not live to see her troops die on that bloody field. She foresaw the defeat and poisoned herself.

Queen Boadicea had her revenge, but it cost Britain dearly. Roman reinforcements were brought in from Germany, and every British tribe and "kingdom" was forced to acknowledge the rule of Rome. There were to be no more "independents" like the Iceni. Furthermore, the tribes were starving. Boadicea had rallied every available man to her army, so that the fields had gone unsown and there were no crops. The famished tribesmen had to bow to their Roman governors and beg food from the Roman storehouses. So all England submitted, and Britain was wholly Roman Britain until the days of King Arthur, some four hundred years later.

LADY GODIVA

According to legend, a later British heroine who defied a tyrant did it in a quite different way. The tyrant was her own husband, but the act he dared her to perform is remembered to this day. You'll certainly recognize her name: Lady Godiva.

In the eleventh century, the town of Coventry and the country thereabout were ruled by Leofric, Earl of Mercia, a harsh and cruel overlord. His gentle wife, Godiva, felt sorry for the people and begged her husband to be kinder to them. He snorted and said sarcastically that he would, on one condition: If Godiva would ride through the market square of Coventry clad in nothing but her long hair. The calculating Leofric fully expected that she'd never do such a thing (ladies simply didn't), but she did!

The people of Coventry were so grateful for Lady Godiva's gesture on their behalf that they stayed indoors on the day she made her naked ride through town, and no one looked out to embarrass her—except one man, a tailor named Thomas, who slyly peeked from his window to gaze upon her bare beauty. The legend says that God struck him blind for it. This act of the tailor put the term "peeping Tom" into our language. Whether there was any other result of Lady Godiva's ride—whether Earl Leofric really reformed —there is no record.

Thomas Becket

A century later, there lived in England a man who became a hero not because he wanted to but because, once he had committed himself to some person or some cause, his loyalty was absolute and unswerving. Not all the causes he championed were entirely admirable, and not all his actions were entirely wise, but his dedication to what he deemed his duty was as heroic as it was stubborn —and it ended only with his death. This was the man who is known to us today as St. Thomas of Canterbury. In his lifetime he was Thomas Becket.

He was thirty-seven years old, in holy orders, and archdeacon of Canterbury, when Henry II came to the English throne in 1155. Henry was only twenty-two years old, and decided he needed an older, more mature counselor to help him rule the land. He appointed Thomas Becket as his Chancellor, and the two immediately became bosom friends. Becket doffed his church vestments and austere sobriety, to don the gaudy costume and grandiloquent manners of the royal court. He and Henry wined, dined, hunted and joked together. They even fought together. During a war with

France, Becket was Henry's second-in-command. He personally led a company of knights and once he himself defeated a champion French knight in hand-to-hand combat. King Henry had no more devoted, brave, intelligent and loyal subject. Thomas Becket was his right-hand man.

Seven years after their first meeting, however, they came to a lamentable parting of the ways.

In Henry's time the Church in England was very nearly as powerful as the crown, and this Henry did not like. Each bishop was not just a spiritual leader; he was the equal of an earl. He usually owned great estates because many nobles bequeathed their lands to the Church, hoping this gesture would help get them into heaven. A bishop could mobilize all the serfs on his estates and put an army in the field. A bishop could excommunicate his enemies at will (that is, deny them all the rites of the Church, even Christian burial, and thus presumably damn their souls to hell), and the bishop's enemies might well be the king's friends.

The highest Church officer in England was the Archbishop of Canterbury, and it was he who appointed all the other bishops. When the old archbishop died in 1162, King Henry saw to it that his comrade Becket was elected to that eminence. Henry assumed that his friend would continue to be loyal and obey him, that he would appoint only manageable bishops—in short, that Becket would make the Church subservient to the crown. In this, Henry was mistaken.

Thomas Becket, as the King's Chancellor, had been devoted to the king. Thomas Becket, as the new Archbishop of Canterbury, was devoted to the Church. Much as it hurt him to oppose his sovereign and long-time friend, Becket was incapable of dividing his devotion; he would do his duty as he saw it. Within a year, Thomas and Henry were no longer on speaking terms. The various disputes which divided them are too complex to go into here—and anyway, the issues involved in Church versus crown have long been settled. Suffice it to say that Becket often successfully stymied Henry's efforts. Those in the middle—the people of England—were the ones who suffered, never knowing which authority to obey, and forever fearful that the pope would strike the country with the Interdict (mass excommunication of everybody).

One day in the winter of 1170, Henry got word of some action of Becket's that he considered especially outrageous. He glared around at the nobles and knights gathered in his throneroom, and snarled, "What a pack of fools and cowards I have nourished in my house, that not one of them will rid me of this turbulent priest!" (Some accounts have it: "this upstart clerk!") Whatever was said, four of Henry's staunchest knights winced at the words, exchanged meaningful glances and slipped unnoticed from the room.

Henry was a law-abiding man, and he had meant only that he wished someone could show him a legal way to unseat Thomas Becket. But, to a warrior knight, getting "rid" of somebody had a different meaning. So these four knights rode full tilt to Canterbury, where they found the archbishop in the cathedral. He stood in the north transept, wearing his priest's garb and holding a cross. The knights came straight to the point: would Becket swear fealty and obedience to Henry? Becket said his faith and obedience were com-

mitted to a greater sovereign, God and His Church. The four drew their swords and hacked him to death.

When Henry heard of this appalling assassination, he was prostrated by grief and horror. Such a sacrilege was unheard of. It endangered his throne, because Becket had been popular with the people. It endangered the souls of his people—and himself. (Indeed, Henry only narrowly averted the pope's pronouncing the dread Interdict.) But, above all, Henry must have remembered the beloved friend with whom he had shared so many rollicking good times. And it was his own unthinking, angry words that had caused his friend's death!

For years thereafter, on every anniversary of the murder, Henry made a pilgrimage to Becket's shrine. There he subjected himself to public penance—the only British monarch ever to abase himself so. He would strip off his shirt, humbly kneel, and let the assembled monks take turns scourging his bare back with a knotted whip. In 1172, Henry made a formal treaty with the pope, agreeing that he would interfere no longer with the powers and privileges of the Church. In that same year, Thomas Becket was canonized as Saint Thomas.

WILLIAM TELL

Almost everyone knows the story of another inadvertent hero, of a century later and of a different country—William Tell, the legendary hunter and crossbowman of Switzerland. Even more familiar is the heroic, galloping music, still often played as a "pop classic," written by Rossini for his opera *William Tell*.

In the year 1291, according to the legend, Switzerland was under the rule of the Habsburgs, Dukes of Austria, and each canton (county or shire) of the little country had an Austrian bailiff appointed to keep order. In William Tell's canton of Uri, the bailiff was a cruel and vindictive man named Gessler. To verify his absolute authority and the abject obedience of his Swiss subjects, Gessler set up a pole in the market square of Uri's chief town, Altdorf, and atop the pole perched the ducal bonnet of the Habsburg family. Every Swiss who entered the square was expected to bow down in salute to this symbol of oppression or else suffer punishment for his defiance.

William Tell was one who refused to bow, and Gessler, in a rage, sentenced Tell to immediate execution unless—and here the tyrant had a vicious inspiration, because Tell was accompanied by his young son Henric—the famous bowman could demonstrate his prowess by shooting an apple off the head of his little boy. Henric stood against a tree at the farthest distance a crossbow could shoot, an apple was placed on his head, and Tell was commanded to fire. Tell raised his bow, stilled his anxiety, and neatly pierced the apple with his quarrel (what a crossbow dart is called). Thus he saved his life and lived to shoot the tyrant Gessler himself sometime later, which precipitated an uprising among the Swiss that swept the Austrian conquerors out of their little country and made them independent at last.

It's a good story, but that's all it is. This one did not begin to be told until some two hundred years after it supposedly happened. In the 1400's, Switzerland really was agitating for full freedom and recognition as a nation. So the Swiss propagandists began inventing and spreading stories like that of William Tell to give the impression that Switzerland's fight for freedom had been going on much longer than it really had.

The concocters of these stories were practical enough to use the names of real people. William Tell and Gessler actually existed at one time, but it is doubtful that a humble peasant hunter and a ducally appointed governor would ever have come face to face, let alone indulge in such a romantic and heroic "duel." Nevertheless, a good story is easy to believe, and today's Swiss will swear that William Tell's legendary feat was the spark that fired them to fight for independence. As a matter of fact, there are "Tell Chapels" here and there in the canton of Uri, commemorating the deed.

Many a man has been acclaimed a hero after his death, not because he ever did anything especially noteworthy, but simply because he was dramatically or unfairly put to death in the prime of life. American Negroes are particularly proud of the fact that the first man to fall in the American Revolution was a black, Crispus Attucks, who was shot in the first brief skirmish between Colonials and British at Lexington, Massachusetts, on April 19, 1775. Poor Attucks never so much as pulled a trigger; his hero status rests on the fact that the affray in which he died has come to be renowned as "the shot heard round the world."

In our own time, the late John F. Kennedy has come to be regarded as a hero mainly because he was assassinated early in his term as President of the United States. He could very well have become one of our greatest Presidents, but he was murdered before he had the opportunity to prove his abilities as President, and so, simply as a martyr who "died in harness," he deserves the respect paid to his memory.

John Huss

More accurately to be defined as heroes are those men who died young because of their beliefs or the causes they upheld. One such was John Huss, or Jan Hus as his name is rendered in his native Bohemia (now part of Czechoslovakia). Had he lived to a ripe old age and a natural death, Huss would have been remembered today as a crusading priest and philosopher—fame enough—but his martyrdom, which he did not seek or expect, elevated him to his status among our inadvertent heroes.

In his short life of 42 years (from 1373 to 1415) Huss campaigned for numerous reforms in the Church of that day and, as a result, was almost always in disfavor with his superiors. For example, he spoke out against the "fake miracles" arranged by other churchmen to bolster the people's faith in Christ. Huss thought it sufficient for the devout "to seek Him in His enduring word." He also declaimed against greedy and power-hungry priests, bishops— and even popes—who abused their authority to the detriment of their flock.

It is not surprising, that Huss was popular with the commonfolk but most unpopular with his Church colleagues. Several times, his superiors forbade him to preach (but he went right on), and once the pope laid the terrible Interdict on the whole city of Prague, where Huss was preaching. When Huss fled into hiding so that the Interdict might be lifted from Prague, the pope instead extended the Interdict to any and every community that might give him shelter. Finally there came a showdown. John Huss was summoned to appear before a Church tribunal in the German city of Constance. Huss would probably have ignored the demand, except that King Sigismund promised him "safe conduct." Whatever the Church council's charges, said the king, Huss would be allowed to return to Bohemia. But Sigismund intended no such thing; he could not afford to flout the power of the Church.

So John Huss, all unsuspecting, walked into the trap. The council denounced him and his preaching as "erroneous, heretical, revolutionary." When Huss stood to make his defense, the assembled churchmen shouted, hissed and booed him into silence. On July 6, 1415, he was sentenced to death, and that very day was led to the stake. As the flames mounted around him, Huss could be heard praying the *Kyrie eleison*—"Lord, have mercy..." Whether he was asking mercy for himself or his persecutors, we shall never know.

When the fire had died, the ashes that were left—and even the soil on which they lay—were scooped up and thrown into the river Rhine.

John Huss died unwillingly, but not in vain. From his burning stake, he can be said to have passed the torch to the next century's Martin Luther (whom you will meet in a later chapter), and Huss' "heretical, revolutionary" ideas helped bring about the Reformation which eventually enabled every man to worship as he, and not the Church, saw fit.

MIGUEL DE CERVANTES

In 1547 was born another man who never intended to be a hero —and he was hardly regarded as such, during his lifetime of drudgery, poverty and even slavery. But he created the immortal Don Quixote, who has become one of the world's great fictional heroes, and whose name is far better remembered than that of his creator, Miguel de Cervantes Saavedra. It is probable that a good many Spaniards and Latin Americans believe to this day that Don Quixote and his sidekick Sancho Panza were once real, living persons.

Actually, Miguel Cervantes had enough heroic adventures of his own that if he'd ever written an autobiography, he might have been acclaimed as a valid—if inadvertent—hero in his own time. At the age of twenty-three he enlisted in the Spanish Army and sailed with an armada against the Turks. Their first battle was fought off the coast of Greece. Cervantes was ill with fever at the time, but insisted on joining in the fight. He received two gunshot wounds in the chest and one which permanently crippled his left hand—"for the greater glory of the right," he used to say afterward, with a grin. His gallantry and his wounds would have been enough to take him honorably out of action, and with a couple of medals, but, after convalescing, he stayed on to fight in several other battles.

When, in 1575, he sailed back to Spain on leave, he carried letters of commendation of his bravery. They were his undoing. The ship on which he was a passenger was captured by Barbary pirates, and all the crew and passengers were sold into slavery in Algiers. Most of the captives were soon released for small ransoms paid by their families. But Cervantes' master, a Greek named Dali Mami, discovered his slave's impressive letters of commendation, decided he was a man of importance, and set his ransom impossibly high. Cervantes' family were poor and it took them fully five years to scrimp, save and borrow the exorbitant ransom.

(In the meantime, Cervantes had several times attempted escape from Algiers, with the result that he was continually being flogged, mistreated and imprisoned.) He finally got home to Spain to find his family and himself impoverished.

He tried to earn a living by writing innumerable poems, plays and a novel—most of them based on his own travels and adventures—but these brought in only a meager income. In 1590, citing his wartime services to the crown, Cervantes managed to get appointed as a sort of auditing clerk to the treasury. (He had to borrow money to buy a suit of clothes in which to report to work.) But he was a terrible businessman. Foolishly, though quite innocently, he kept getting his accounts muddled, and every time he did he was thrown into prison. It was during one of these terms behind bars that he began drafting his *Don Quixote de la Mancha*.

By this period, those European novels, poems and ballads of the Age of Chivalry (which had inspired Malory with much of the material for the King Arthur legend) had become *so* absurd and flowery—teeming with knights gallant to the point of stupidity, unbelievable dragons, monsters and ogres, wispy and weepy maidens, lovers forever dying of heartbreak, and so on—that Cervantes wrote his book mainly to poke fun at all this claptrap.

His Don Quixote, an elderly gent of rather addled brains, who has read and believed too many of these preposterous romances, sets out, with his faithful but boneheaded squire Sancho Panza, to save all those maidens in distress and vanquish all those impossible villains. The two meet with extravagant adventures—mostly misadventures—in which the foolish but idealistic old knight comes off much the worse for wear.

But *Don Quixote de la Mancha* turned out to be far more than a burlesque. Its characters came to life under Cervantes' pen. He sketched the whole fabric of sixteenth-century Spanish life; incidents both humorous and pathetic; recognizable people of high and low degree—nobles, knights, poets, priests, traders, farmers, muleskinners, scullions, convicts, country girls, kitchen wenches, gypsies—in short, the book was a panorama of his country and his times.

Miguel Cervantes was nearly sixty when his book was published. The Spanish people immediately took the book to their hearts—and seem immediately to have accepted "the knight of the woeful countenance" and every other character as real people existing somewhere in the local countryside. They also begged for a sequel. A hack writer named Avellaneda obligingly came out with *The Second Book of the Ingenious Don Quixote,* far inferior to Cervantes' work. It was probably to disown that imitation that Cervantes buckled down to write his own Volume II of the knight's adventures. Also, although the first volume had won him celebrity and had been translated into four other languages, it had failed to earn him much money.

After the second book appeared and added to Cervantes' fame, it inspired a special mission of French literary men to travel to Madrid to meet the genius who had written these masterpieces. They were astounded to hear that he was "old, a soldier, a gentleman, and poor." Cervantes continued to write until his death— his last act on the last day of his life was to add the dedication to his last novel. He died (five days before William Shakespeare died) still so poor that his widow could afford no headstone for his grave, and today his resting place cannot be located. It has been said that Cervantes' earlier works would have made him the foremost of Spanish writers, but his *Don Quixote* ranks him with the greatest writers of all nations and all times. "Children turn its leaves, young people read it, grown men understand it, old folk praise it." Cervantes never set out to be a hero—he was no mighty conqueror of countries—but he captured the hearts of all the world through his immortal masterpiece.

Chief Joseph

Another hero whose fame rests on his unforgettable words along with the actions which inspired them was an American Indian named Heinmot Tooyalaket, better known as "Chief Joseph" of the Nez Percé tribe. This tribe received its name ("those of the pierced noses") from the early French fur trappers who were impressed by the shell ornaments the Indian wore in their noses. Those same French trappers also found the tribe hospitable and kindly disposed toward the white men. So did American explorers Meriwether Lewis and William Clark when, during their epic Western trek of 1804 and 1806, they stumbled starving and sick into the Nez Percé country, to be welcomed, fed, restored to health and helped on their way to the Pacific.

The Nez Percés were *too* hospitable, in fact. When white settlers began moving into their territory in what is now western Idaho, southeastern Washington and northeastern Oregon, the Indians gave ground before them. Eventually the Nez Percé tribe had no territory to call its own but the Valley of Winding Waters in Oregon—and then the whites decided they wanted that land, too. In 1877, the tribe was ordered to pick up and move to a small reservation in Idaho. Then, for the first time, the Nez Percés refused, and General O. O. Howard was sent to move them. Howard gave Chief Joseph just thirty days to decamp or be removed by force.

Joseph's tribe numbered only about seven hundred Indians, and only two hundred and fifty of them were warriors; the rest were old folk, women and children. He could not possibly oppose the whole U.S. Army, so the Indians gathered their horses and packed them with their belongings. They had time to round up only a fraction of their cattle grazing throughout the valley. When they got to the Snake River, they found it a raging torrent, swollen by melting snows. Somehow they got their women, children and packs across the river on buffalo-hide rafts. But while they were thus engaged, and their cattle were waiting to be herded across, a party of white men stole a good portion of the herd.

Chief Joseph pushed the tribe along, though several angry young braves wanted to stop and take revenge for their ouster and the loss and theft of their stock. When the tribe halted for a rest in Rocky Canyon, those braves did slip away and killed eleven white settlers—the first time a Nez Percé had ever harmed a white. Chief Joseph was saddened and alarmed, because he knew what this would mean. General Howard immediately charged that the Indians had gone on the warpath, and sent troops on their trail to wipe them out.

Joseph changed direction, heading toward the buffalo country of Montana. On the way, his warriors fought and won many rearguard actions against the pursuing soldiers. Several times, when they camped to rest, the Indians were attacked in force. They lost many women and children as well as braves, but each time the troops were driven off. In addition to Howard's soldiers on the Indians' trail, the Army Commander called in the Seventh Cavalry from the Dakota Territory to intersect their line of march and cut them off from any possibility of making a stand in Montana.

Chief Joseph realized that the only hope of his tribe—or what was left of it—was to escape entirely from the United States. He turned north toward kinder Canada. The U.S. Army scouts reported the move, so still another force was called in, under General Nelson Miles, to cut off that route as well. The Nez Percés, harried by attacks along the way, burdened with their noncombatant families, driving a herd of cattle, and traveling on foot (because their horses were carrying what pitifully few possessions they owned), had traversed 1,300 miles in four months, and were just one day's march from the Canadian border and safety when General Miles intercepted them.

For four days, the Nez Percés held off the repeated charges of 600 cavalrymen, killing two troopers for every brave they lost. But this could not continue; the braves were too few and getting fewer. On the fifth day, Chief Joseph surrendered his rifle to General Miles as a token of their surrender.

Now the Nez Percés were denied even the reservation in Idaho. They were sent instead to absolutely "foreign" country: the Indian Territory of what is now Oklahoma. They were exiled in that alien land, among strange Indians, until 1885, by which time Chief Joseph's pleading got the remaining Nez Percés—there were only 287 left by then—transferred to that promised Idaho reserve. Chief Joseph and some other tribal leaders, however, were considered "too dangerous" to be given such freedom. They were condemned to a reservation—really a concentration camp—in the state of Washington, and there Chief Joseph died "of a broken heart" in 1904.

He is remembered for his words. Chief Joseph's speech of surrender to General Miles is one of the most eloquent addresses ever made by an Indian. Here, in English translation, is the gist of it:

"I am tired of fighting. Our chiefs are killed. The old men are all dead. It is cold and we have no blankets. The little children are freezing to death. My people, some of them, have run away to the hills, and have no blankets, no food. No one knows where they are. I want to have time to look for my children. Maybe I shall find them among the dead. Hear me, my chiefs! I am tired; my heart is sick and sad. From where the sun now stands, I will fight no more forever."

ANNE FRANK

Our final inadvertent hero or heroine is known only through her words. The pivotal and heroic twenty-five months of her life were spent hiding in an attic in Amsterdam, capital of the Netherlands, never emerging into the outside world. All that has survived from that time and all that we know of her is in her diary. Among the several books given to her as presents on her thirteenth birthday, June 12, 1942, was a blank diary. She immediately began writing in it—she addressed each entry to an imaginary "Kitty," as if the diary were a girl friend; she had no other—and to it she confided the experiences, hopes, beliefs, thoughts of almost every day of the rest of her life. The girl's name was Anne Frank. Here is a typical entry:

"Dear Kitty: It's an odd idea for someone like me to keep a diary . . . because it seems to me that neither I—nor for that matter anyone else—will be interested in the unbosomings of a thirteen-year-old schoolgirl. Still, what does that matter? I want to write, but more than that, I want to bring out all kinds of things that lie buried deep in my heart."

Two years earlier, in 1940, the Nazi armies had invaded and overrun the Netherlands. There had then begun, under the Nazi governors and their Dutch collaborators, a reign of terror for the Dutch Jews, including the Frank family. Every Jew had to wear a six-pointed yellow star prominently displayed on his clothing. Jews had to surrender their cars and bicycles, and were banned

from trains. Jews were allowed to shop only between three and five o'clock each afternoon, and then only in Jewish shops. Jews had to be indoors by eight o'clock. Jews were forbidden to visit theaters, movie houses, swimming pools, and other places of entertainment. Jewish children had to attend Jewish schools. Jews were not allowed to visit Christians.

Then, in July, 1942, the most vicious wing of the Nazi Army, the dreaded SS troops, began their "call-ups" of Dutch Jews to be sent to concentration camps. Of the 112,000 Jews who lived in the Netherlands at the beginning of the Second World War, 104,000 died in those camps. Anne's father, Otto Frank, determined to hide himself, his wife, their daughters Margot (sixteen) and Anne (thirteen), and their closest friends, Mr. and Mrs. Van Daan and their son Peter (fifteen).

"5 *July 1942*
" . . . Margot and I began to pack some of our most vital belongings in a school satchel. The first thing I put in was this diary. . . . I put in the craziest things . . . but I'm not sorry; memories mean more to me than dresses. We put on heaps of clothes as if we were going to the North Pole, the sole reason being to take clothes with us. No Jew in our situation would have dreamed of going out with a suitcase. At seven-thirty the door closed behind us . . . "

Otto Frank owned a business in downtown Amsterdam, and his building was part offices and part warehouse. At the very top were five tiny rooms and an attic. These could be blocked off and the stairway to them camouflaged. For more than two years, from early July of 1942, it was the home—no, it was the whole world—of the Franks and the Van Daans. The only other people who knew of the Secret Annex (as they came to call it) were Frank's four faithful Christian employees, who continued to run the business downstairs.

"11 *July 1942*
" . . . The Secret Annex is an ideal hiding place. Although it leans to one side and is damp, you'd never find such a comfortable hiding place anywhere. Even so, sounds could travel through the walls. We have forbidden Margot to cough at night, although she has a bad cold. . . . I can't tell you how oppressive it is *never* to be able to go outdoors."

They had to subsist on food smuggled in by non-Jewish friends, and there wasn't much of that. Food was strictly rationed and, as they were no longer legally in existence, the Franks and Van Daans naturally had no ration books. Nevertheless, Anne realized how much better off they were than many other Jews.

"19 November 1942
". . . Countless friends and acquaintances have gone to a terrible fate. Evening after evening the green and gray army trucks trundle past. The Germans ring at every front door to inquire if there are any Jews living in the house. It seems like the slave hunts of olden times."

Still, Anne was human, and sometimes she couldn't help confiding her distress to "Kitty."

"25 December 1943
". . . Cycling, dancing, whistling, looking out into the world, feeling young, to know that I'm free—that's what I long for. I sometimes ask myself: Would anyone, either Jew or non-Jew, understand this about me, that I am simply a young girl badly in need of some rollicking fun? I don't know, and I couldn't talk about it to anyone, because then I know I should cry."

It might be supposed that a normal, vivacious teenager would have gone insane in that dungeon of enforced closeness, with no exercise, no entertainment, no diversion, and not even a vestige of privacy. But the Secret Annex did at least have books, and Anne was a more than normally intelligent and disciplined youngster.

"11 May 1944
". . . I'm frightfully busy at the moment, and although it sounds mad, I haven't time to get through my pile of work. Shall I tell you briefly what I have got to do? Well then, by tomorrow I must finish reading the first part of *Galileo Galilei*. I only started it yesterday, but I shall manage it. Next week I have got to read *Palestine at the Crossroads*. I finished reading the first part of the biography of *The Emperor Charles V* yesterday, and it's essential that I work out all the diagrams and family trees that I have collected from it. Next: Theseus, Oedipus, Peleus, Orpheus, Jason and Hercules are all awaiting their turn to be arranged, as their different deeds lie crisscross in my

mind like fancy threads in a dress. Oh, something else, the Bible. What do they mean by the guilt of Sodom and Gomorrah? Oh, there is still such a terrible lot to find out and to learn!"

It is good that young Anne had food for thought, because she and the other hideaways got less and less food to eat. The occupation authorities repeatedly cut down on the food rations, and even non-Jews were tightening their belts.

"25 May 1944
". . . Mummy says she shall cut out breakfast altogether, have porridge and bread for lunch, and for supper fried potatoes, and possibly once or twice per week vegetables or lettuce, nothing more. We're going to be hungry, but anything is better than being discovered."

And then, over their hidden and muffled little radio, they heard a long-awaited and electrifying bulletin.

"6 June 1944
". . . 'This is D-day,' came the announcement over the English news. The invasion has begun! Hope is revived within us; it gives us fresh courage, and makes us strong again. Now more than ever we must clench our teeth and not cry out. We have been oppressed by these terrible Germans for so long that the thought of friends and deliverance fills us with confidence!"

A week later, Anne wrote:

"13 June 1944
". . . Another birthday has gone by, so now I'm fifteen."

She was never to be sixteen. On August 4, 1944, before the Allied armies could liberate the Netherlands, five Nazi patrolmen, on a routine search of the building, discovered the hidden stairway and raided the Secret Annex. All the hideaways, plus the office employees who had concealed their presence, were arrested and sent to concentration camps. In March of 1945, in the unspeakable camp of Bergen-Belsen, and barely two months before Germany surrendered and the war ended, Anne Frank died.

When the patrolmen routed out the Franks and Van Daans, their orders were to sweep the hideout clean and to leave no trace of their ugly deed. But they failed in that. They overlooked Anne's diary— stark evidence of the inhumanity of the Nazis and their collaborators —poignant evidence that not all their might, not even murder, could quench the spirit of one tender but enduring young soul. Anne Frank's words live on. One of the very last entries she addressed to "Kitty" was this:

"15 July 1944
". . . It's really a wonder that I haven't dropped all my ideals, because they seem so absurd and impossible to carry out. Yet I keep them, because in spite of everything I still believe that people are really good at heart."

(*AUTHOR'S NOTE:* The quotations from Anne Frank's diary are from *Anne Frank, The Diary of a Young Girl,* translated by B. M. Mooyart, and published by Doubleday & Co., Garden City, N.Y. in 1952; revised edition, 1967.)

Conquerors and Founders

See, the conquering hero comes!
Sound the trumpet, beat the drums!
—Thomas Morell

The conqueror of an existing nation or the founder of a new one is not always universally beloved or regarded as a hero. Obviously, for every great victory that one people celebrates, another people must mourn a great defeat. For every new nation founded, some other nation is either subdued or evicted. For every new throne or new god set up, an older one is toppled. And yet, although we may deplore some of their aims or methods, the conquerors and founders are true heroes—in that they possess such overwhelming abilities, ambitions or dynamic personalities that they inspire legions of other men to help them rearrange the map, the languages spoken, the laws and religions observed. The world as we know it today was shaped by these men.

ALEXANDER THE GREAT

One of the greatest conquerors of history was not, like most warriors of his era, just a barbarian with no ability other than brute

89

force. Instead, he was intelligent, gifted and well-educated, in addition to being brave and ambitious. He was Alexander III, better known as Alexander the Great.

Alexander was born in 356 B.C., the son of King Philip II of Macedon (the country just north of Greece in ancient times), and he was brought up in true princely style, his tutor being the Greek sage Aristotle, still considered to be one of the wisest philosophers who ever lived. Alexander might well have been overshadowed by his father—because Philip had grandiose plans of his own for world conquest—but the king was assassinated, and Alexander took the throne at the age of twenty. As if he knew that he had little time to make a name for himself—only thirteen years, as it turned out—Alexander immediately led his army surging forth from Macedon.

At that time the numerous city-states of Greece were warring among themselves. Alexander marched there on the pretext of settling these petty squabbles. And settle them he did, by taking over all the city-states one by one—no difficult task, since they were too busy harrying each other to unite against him. Next he went to settle some minor uprisings in the lands of Illyria and Thrace—and he settled them in the same way, by total conquest. At the age of twenty-two, Alexander was the acknowledged ruler of most of what was then "civilized Europe"—what is now Albania, Greece, Bulgaria, European Turkey, and the southern half of Yugoslavia.

That wasn't enough, however. His father Philip had long planned on sending an army into Asia to make war on Persia. Alexander decided to do it as a memorial to him. He began by crossing the strait between Europe and what is now Asiatic Turkey. When he swept into the land of Phrygia, legend says that the Phrygians awaited him unafraid, trusting in the power of their "Gordian knot." This was a fist-sized intricate knot in a rope made of twisted bark, contrived by a long-dead Phrygian king named Gordius. An oracle had declared that the country would never be conquered except by one who could untie the Gordian knot. Over the years countless men—from would-be conquerors to just curious passers-by—had tried to untie it and failed. Alexander came, looked at the knot, drew his sword and slashed it in twain. He had indeed undone the Gordian knot, and the Phrygians surrendered to him on the spot. A minor incident, but it shows the man. A problem that others might fiddle with he solved with one bold stroke.

With the same boldness and unwavering purpose, Alexander moved on through Asia. In turn, he conquered Phoenicia, the long-time sea rival of the Greek merchants; he defeated the last of the Persian kings, ending an empire that had endured for some six hundred years; he detoured into Egypt and subdued it so that the people acclaimed him "son and heir" of the ancient pharaohs; he conquered Bactria and Sogdiana, comprising what is now Afghanistan —pausing there long enough to marry a Bactrian princess named Roxana. (This is interesting because more than sixteen hundred years later, the much-traveled explorer Marco Polo was to describe the Bactrian women as "the most beautiful in the world.") Alexander did not stop until his army had conquered the Punjab region of India.

Legend says that, while there in the far Himalaya Mountains, Alexander sat and wept because "there are no more worlds to conquer." He realized that the many lands he had conquered would not remain his unless he remolded their governments, laws and loyalties. So he decreed that all the conquered peoples must be taught the Greek language, Greek manners, and Greek customs as he had learned from Aristotle. Alexander's soldiers were to become schoolmasters, and every military outpost from the Aegean Sea to the Himalaya Mountains was to become a model Greek city-in-miniature for the new subjects to admire and imitate.

Soon after Alexander had explained this plan to his commanders he fell ill of a fever and died—at the early age of thirty-three. He had won and ruled an empire far more vast than any ever known before him. Almost immediately upon his death, however, that empire began to dissolve. Several of his ambitious generals joined in carving it up among themselves. But they too were Greek in outlook, and attempted to carry on Alexander's dream of spreading Greek ideas, arts and knowledge.

The several regions remained separate until the Roman Empire absorbed them about three hundred years later. Rome also absorbed their mixed Greek-Persian-Egyptian-Babylonian culture and disseminated it throughout the rest of the empire. Our present western world owes much of *its* culture to the Roman world. So, to this very day, our lives are influenced by Alexander's conquests—which were not just conquests of an assortment of nations and peoples, but of those peoples' minds as well.

Julius Caesar

The man who laid the foundations of the Roman Empire was Julius Caesar, in the first century B.C. Unlike Alexander, he did not start his wars of conquest until he was about forty-five years old.

Before that, he had held numerous political positions and had devised the Julian calendar, a great improvement over the older calendar inherited from the Egyptians, which was so inaccurate that in Julius' time January was falling in autumn. Caesar, after a term as governor of the Roman province of Spain, became one of the triumvirate who were three equal rulers of the Republic of Rome. The other two were Crassus and Pompey. Crassus was killed in a minor war, and thereafter Pompey and Caesar jealously vied for pre-eminence.

Caesar decided to go for glory. Despite his (for those days) fairly advanced age, in 58 B.C. he took an army across the Alps into central Europe and began the Gallic Wars. He conquered Gaul (what is now France). Then he built a wooden bridge across the "uncrossable" Rhine River and conquered much of what is now Germany. Finally, he recrossed Europe and then crossed the English Channel, to start the occupation of England. There's no knowing where he might have gone next, but his conquests had already made him such a popular hero back in Rome that the envious Senate sent word to Caesar that he was relieved of his army command.

Caesar wasn't about to step down from his heroic pedestal. Every man in his army adored him (it is said that he knew every soldier by name), and they swore to follow him in whatever action he took. Caesar marched back through Europe and crossed the Rubicon, the stream bounding his province, to enter into Pompey's home domain. The expression "to cross the Rubicon" still means to make a fateful and irrevocable decision.

All this meant civil war, but with his own army and the Roman people solidly behind him, Caesar had no trouble unseating Pompey, who fled with his own forces to Greece. Caesar was unanimously elected sole leader of the republic. Then he and his army marched again, to defeat Pompey and his troops; to put down some small rebellions in Spain; then to Egypt, which he made an ally by indulging in a love affair with its Queen Cleopatra. Finally he easily conquered Syria, which at that time included most of the Middle East. It was from there that he sent his famous and laconic message: *veni, vidi, vici*—"I came, I saw, I conquered."

At last back in Rome, he set about consolidating his newly-won empire, which now included practically all the "world" that was known at that time. His new laws were so sweeping and novel and admirable—among them, one making Roman citizens of even the far-away subjects—that Rome elected him dictator for life. This did not sit too well with many of his subordinates, who saw themselves forever barred from advancement. On the Ides of March (the fifteenth of the month, according to Caesar's own calendar) in 44 B.C., a group of conspirators—including former friends and followers Antony and Brutus—waylaid him on the steps of the Senate and stabbed him to death.

Caesar's demise did not, however, restore the republic. His 18-year-old grandnephew Octavian followed him as ruler (taking the name Augustus Caesar) and he was succeeded by other despotic rulers. The republic was no more, Rome was now an empire which dominated the known world for another four hundred years, until the Romans lapsed into self-indulgent decadence and became too weak to resist the assaults of northern barbarians, the Goths and Huns. The empire then lost its outlying provinces, one after another, and finally the regal city of Rome itself fell to the barbarians.

But Julius Caesar, architect of the empire, was never forgotten. Caesar had been merely a family name, like Jones or Jennings, until Julius made it famous. Thereafter, every one of his successors took Caesar as the title of his position, and it was perpetuated all the way down to modern times. Until the First World War, the Germans called their ruler not king or emperor but *Kaiser*, and the Russians called their ruler the *Tsar*—both words being adaptations of "Caesar."

CHARLEMAGNE

By the time of the fall of Rome in A.D. 476, its European provinces were already in fragments. Hispania (Spain) had been partitioned out amongst the Moors (who invaded from Africa) and the native Asturians and Basques (these latter, Rome had never been able to subdue, nor has any conqueror since). Gaul, or France, was split among numerous Celtic tribes. Germania, or Germany, was divided among Franks, Saxons and Lombards. Still, all these peoples—even the insignificant "kings" of the many midget "kingdoms"—wistfully believed that the Roman Empire had merely been suspended, not ended, and that it would be united in all its might again someday.

And so it was—but briefly, however, and not until more than three hundred years later—and then through the efforts of a Frankish chieftain called Charlemagne. We might deem him a barbarian: he could barely read, never learned to write and, though he preferred Latin to his native Germanic tongue, he had trouble learning to speak it. Yet, for all his ignorance and his savagery in war, Charlemagne had quite civilized and forward-looking ideas.

In battle after battle, he first brought Gaul under his control, and then Germania. He went into Spain to battle the Moorish invaders, but he was balked in that, because the native Basques also resented his butting-in, and they inflicted on Charlemagne the only major defeat of his career. This battle also made a legendary hero of Roland, one of Charlemagne's twelve paladins, or noble subcommanders. To cover the retreat of the main body of Charlemagne's army, Roland and a handful of his men volunteered for the suicide mission of staying and holding a pass in the Pyrenees, the mountain range between France and Spain. They died to a man, but they held off the Basques long enough for the army to get safely through and into Gaul.

At this period in history, Christianity had become a recognized religion, and had long been administered by a pope at Rome. Charlemagne was a Christian, and greatly helped to spread the religion by demanding that every pagan people he conquered should convert to Christianity. In the year 795, a new pope, Leo III, was elected, but he was most unpopular with the people of Rome. Indeed, he **was** ambushed in the streets and beaten nearly to death. He recovered, however, and fled to the Frankish town where Charlemagne was then encamped.

Charlemagne sent an army of his Franks to restore order in Rome, and then accompanied Leo back to the city. With the help of Charlemagne's "police force," Leo was able to establish himself securely on the papal throne. In the year 800, on Christmas Day, Pope Leo III summoned Charlemagne to the supreme cathedral of Christendom, the church of St. Peter, and there formally crowned him *Imperator Augustus, i.e,* "August Emperor of the Holy Roman Empire"—a title that had not been used or heard for more than three hundred years.

During the remaining years of his life, Charlemagne built towns and monasteries all over northern Europe. He permitted the peoples he had conquered to retain their own customs and laws, and helped them enforce those laws. He diminished the tyrannical power of petty nobles and increased the rights of their subjects. He campaigned for widespread education for all his people (to be taught in the Latin tongue). In short, he proved a wise and good ruler. But this new Roman Empire was not destined to last. Charlemagne died at the age of seventy-two, in the year 814, and his sons and grandsons, after a long quarrel over supremacy, finally in 870 settled on a treaty that divided Charlemagne's domain into two parts—more or less what are now France and Germany.

Even during Charlemagne's lifetime, the northern coast of his Gaul and Germania were being harried by the long ships of the Norsemen (or Vikings) of Scandinavia. Charlemagne had planned to build a mighty sea force and exterminate these pests, but he died before he could put his plan into action, and in the bickerings, confusion and partition after his death, the plan was forgotten. So the Norsemen, unopposed, made ever bolder and more formidable assaults.

In the year 910, one of Charlemagne's distant successors, the king of what had now become France, Charles III—who was known, not without reason, as Charles the Simple—arranged a parley with the most belligerent of the Norsemen, a chieftain named Rollo. He said, in effect, "Look, Rollo, I'll give you a piece of my kingdom if you'll stop ravaging the rest of it." Rollo agreed, and forthwith became ruler of a good-sized hunk of France. Today that province again belongs to France, but its name (derived from the Norsemen) is still Normandy.

WILLIAM THE CONQUEROR

Settling and prospering in Normandy kept Rollo and his descendants peaceably occupied for several generations—though other Viking bands continued to rove the seas and make life precarious for their victims along the coasts of Europe, Russia and the British Isles. By the time Rollo's great-grandson, William, had become in his turn Duke of Normandy, life in Normandy was too settled and quiet to suit him. William looked across the English Channel at England, one of the favorite looting-and-pillaging grounds of his seafaring ancestors, and England looked to him ripe for attention again.

Quite fortuitously, at about this time the English Harold, then Earl of Wessex, while on a Channel voyage, was shipwrecked on the Normandy coast. He was brought to William's court and received with unexpected hospitality. William told Harold that he would not imprison and hold him for ransom—as was customary procedure with distinguished foreign prisoners—but would let him go back to England in return for Harold's promise to aid William if and when he might make a bid for the English crown. Harold said he'd certainly do what he could, and William sent him on his way.

Just two years later when the old king died, what Harold did, however, was to get himself crowned King of England. This infuriated William, who gathered an army and a transport fleet and sailed across the Channel. In October of 1066, he defeated and slew Harold at the Battle of Hastings. On Christmas Day, William the Conqueror was crowned King of England.

William is the only conqueror to wear the title Conqueror as part of his name. He wore it proudly, and with good reason, for he had to keep on conquering during most of his reign. The Britons—by this time a mixture of Anglo-Saxon-Celtic-Roman-Danish—did not take kindly to having a Norman-Frenchman as their ruler. William had to roam the island, putting down one unruly faction after another. But he succeeded, and his success involved more than that. Ever since King Arthur's time, England had been a motley aggregation of what were practically separate little countries. Before William, the King of England had been only a feeble token ruler. Each separate earl ruled his own extensive lands, commanded the loyalty of his tenants, had his own private army, and so on. For the king to declare war against a common enemy or levy a tax, or make almost any decision at all, he first had to consult with and get the cooperation of at least a majority of his nobles.

William changed all this. The nobles who would not swear fealty and obedience to him were simply removed, and in their place he installed Norman knights that he could count on for support (most of them being related to him). When William finished conquering England, about 1072, he was the undisputed ruler of all. And from William's conquest down to quite recent times, the King of England has been *the King*, and his writ has run the length and breadth of the land. After William, there were weak kings, wicked kings, even lunatic kings, who did England no good and sometimes did great harm. But there were strong monarchs, too, both kings and queens, and thanks to William's having secured absolute power for the crown, they made England the most influential country in the western world since the heyday of Rome.

JENGHIZ KHAN

As we said earlier, a conqueror is a hero to his (winning) side and almost always is loathed as a villain by the losers. No man better illustrates this than Jenghiz Khan, the most vicious and unstoppable conqueror of all time. He was a hero only to the warriors of his native Mongol tribe with whom he first sallied forth, about 1206, from an obscure area in what is now Siberia. His so-called Golden Horde eventually numbered in the hundreds of thousands, but to millions of other people, Jenghiz Khan was a villain. In just one city, the Khan's men butchered 1,600,000 innocent civilians—men, women and children. Altogether, he leveled to the ground eight major cities, plus innumerable towns, villages and military strongholds. Even when the people surrendered without a fight, they were put to the sword. The complete death toll of Jenghiz Khan's victims is incalculable. He is worth mention here only because he was the most implacable conqueror of all time (he was never defeated), and his empire was bigger than any one man has ever ruled before or since his time.

Jenghiz Khan's name was originally Temuchin. He was thirteen when his father died, leaving him chief of just one of the many Mongol tribes. When he grew to manhood, however, he led his tribe's warriors on a campaign to subdue and gather all the other Mongols under his flag. Then he took the name Jenghiz Khan—in the Mongol tongue *Chingiz*, meaning "perfect warrior," while *khan* is an old oriental word for "ruler."

His armies thundered out of their obscure region of northern Asia,

going to the south, east and west, and laying waste to the world as they went. There is no need to detail their ferocious battles, their mass murders, their looting, pillaging and other atrocities. It is enough to know that the Mongol warrior was a superb horseman, swordsman and archer, absolutely without fear of death, merciless toward any enemy. Whenever Jenghiz conquered a city and all its inhabitants had been slain, it was his custom to mount some high tower (if any such thing was still standing) and bellow, "The hay is cut! Give your horses fodder!" That was the signal for his men to start plundering everything of value they could find.

With such men and such tactics, Jenghiz Khan conquered what is now Mongolia, China, most of Siberia, the whole southern half of what is now Asiatic Russia. He didn't stop until he reached the Dnieper River in European Russia. His domain stretched from the Dnieper in Europe to the China Sea shore of Asia—some 6,500 miles from west to east, and perhaps 1,000 miles from north to south, about 6,500,000 square miles in all. Now, the entire earth (discounting bleak areas like the Antarctic and the Sahara) has about 50,000,000 square miles of habitable land. Figure it out: Jenghiz Khan owned thirteen per cent of the whole planet's living space.

Then, in 1227, aged sixty-five, he died. His body was carried with great ceremony to the sacred Altai Mountains in Mongolia for burial. Whenever the procession encountered some traveler on the road, one of the attendants would cry, "Depart for the next world to serve your dead master!"—and behead the luckless person. This became a custom and pattern for all future khans: burial in the Altai, and to take along in death whatever people they met on the way. It is said that when Mangu Khan died in 1294, a hundred days' journey from the Altai, the warriors accompanying his coffin slew 20,000 persons on the road.

The reign of terror of the Golden Horde was a nightmare, but, on the time-scale of history, it also passed as quickly as a nightmare. Jenghiz Khan's descendants proved less able than he. They let the far-flung empire shrink until it comprised only China, and this they held only until 1368, when they were deposed by another dynasty. Today our world has only two surviving reminders of the Golden Horde: Their native area of northern Asia, now divided between Russia and China, is still named Mongolia. And, because Jenghiz Khan chased the ancestors of the Turks from their Central Asia homeland clear to the shores of the Mediterranean, Turkey now extends a little way into Europe.

HERNÁN CORTÉS

Jenghiz Khan had several hundred thousand horsemen to help him make his vast conquests. But there was another conqueror who dared to invade a totally unknown territory of some 33 million population—at least a million of them trained and well-experienced warriors—while leading just five hundred and eight men armed with crossbows, muskets and swords, sixteen horses and fourteen light-weight cannon. The territory was what is today Mexico. The man was Hernán Cortés.

After Columbus discovered America, the Spanish made the island of Cuba their base for other exploration in the New World. One explorer had determined that Florida was not an island and that there was a tremendous continent to the north of Cuba. In 1518, another exploring ship reported that there was also a tremendous continent to the west. Later that year, the governor of Cuba outfitted ten ships and picked a minor but ambitious official, Hernán Cortés, to lead an expedition to that land.

Cortés was, like all of Spain's *conquistadores* (conquerors), daring, valiant and determined. He also had audacity and cunning—qualities he found necessary on this expedition. For example, when his ten ships anchored near what is now Veracruz, he knew that as soon as his few hundred soldiers realized what a boundless land they were in and how many "Indians" they were expected to conquer, they could be expected to quail at the prospect. So, when they were ashore, Cortés boldly set fire to the ships and burned nine of them to the waterline. He left his men with no escape and no alternative but to push on into the interior.

There was one other thing Cortés needed: an incredible amount of good luck—and he had that, too. It so happened that the country's natives believed in a number of gods. Among these was Quetzalcoatl, who supposedly had long before lived on earth among them. He had sailed away in a boat into the Gulf and eastward, promising to return some day. Now there had come this whole fleet of "floating houses" out of the east, full of white-skinned, bearded beings, with guns and horses which the indigenes had never seen before. The leader just had to be the god Quetzalcoatl, returning as promised!

For this reason, Cortés at first met only token resistance from a few tribes as he and his men began the mountainous climb into the interior. Along the way, he learned from the indigenes that the foremost ruler in the country was the "Chief Speaker" of the tribe called Mexica. His name was Motecuhzoma (the Spaniards made that Montezuma, and mistakenly called his tribe Aztecs). He dwelt in the fabulous white city of Tenochtitlan; he commanded the fiercest soldiers of any ruler, and had become wealthy and powerful by demanding tribute from the weaker tribes. Cortés also learned that these other tribes, through whose territories he was marching, did not like paying tribute to Motecuhzoma, and would be glad to see him overthrown. From each tribe along the way, Cortés enlisted scores or hundreds or thousands of men eager to help conquer the Mexica. By the time Cortés had climbed the last mountain pass and looked down on the city of Tenochtitlan, he was leading, besides his Spaniards, some 30,000 indigene warriors and porters.

Tenochtitlan was built on two islands in the middle of an extensive lake. It was as big and beautiful as any city the Spaniards had seen—laced with canals, towering with temples and pyramids, overflowing with flowers. Cortés knew that if he could take this magnificent city, all the rest of the country would recognize his power and would be easy to conquer. For a while it did look as if Cortés could take Tenochtitlan without firing a shot. When he crossed on one of the three causeways linking the mainland to the island city, Motecuhzoma received him with open gates and open arms, still half-believing this ordinary-looking man to be the returned god.

Once inside the city, Cortés repaid Motecuhzoma's hospitality by making him a prisoner in his own palace and demanding all the gold in his treasury. Cortés and his men got the gold, but then realized that they were as much prisoners as Motecuhzoma. Their indigene allies had camped on the mainland, and here the Spaniards were, in a palace compound deep inside the city, on an island in a lake surrounded by an immense and alien country. The city's 300,000 people were outraged at the Spaniards' treatment of their ruler, and maybe one-tenth of those people were warriors armed with obsidian-edged swords and lances.

One of Cortés' lieutenants, mistaking a religious fiesta for an uprising, ordered his men to fire on the crowd—and then they did have an uprising on their hands. Cortés, although reinforced by some 800 additional musketeers sent from Cuba, found himself besieged. Under cover of night, he led his troops in a dash for safety, and discovered that the Mexica had cut all the causeways leading from the city to the mainland. The Spaniards bridged the gaps with hastily thrown-together materials, but meanwhile suffered heavy losses. These were caused as much by their own greed as by the swords of the Mexica, because many a man fell into the water and sank like a stone, weighted down by the stolen gold he carried.

Cortés escaped, but with only about half of his men. Once across the lake and given sanctuary by a friendly tribe miles away, however, Cortés gathered another native army, this time numbering 200,000. He determined to attack Tenochtitlan both by land and by water. He had his indigene allies build him thirteen sailing brigs, half-size replicas of the warships in which he had come from Cuba. These brigs were dismantled and carried, piece by piece, overland to the lake, and there reseassembled and launched. It was one of the most novel, daring and brilliant ideas ever hatched by a conqueror.

This time the city stood not a chance, though it held out for eighty days under bombardment from the lake and repeated attacks along the causeways. Four out of five of the city's people were killed and, as Cortés advanced, he had every building torn to the ground so that it wouldn't serve as a vantage for an ambush. When finally he set fire to the city's greatest temple, on August 12, 1521, the Mexica surrendered. Tenochtitlan had vanished from the earth.

Conquering the rest of the country was little more than a lengthy mopping-up operation, while the new Spanish-style city of Mexico was rising from the ruins of Tenochtitlan and the resident Spaniards were importing their wives and families from Cuba and Spain. King Carlos V ennobled Cortés as the Marquis del Valle, appointed him governor of this New Spain, and gave him vast lands (and indigene slaves) for his personal estates.

But Cortés had enemies, envious of his success, in both Old Spain and New Spain, and they poisoned the king's mind against him. He was removed as governor, his authority was gradually diminished, his lands were whittled away, his wealth confiscated on this and that pretext. Finally Cortés returned to Spain to plead his case; but he was no diplomat. He introduced himself to the king with the untactful remark that "I am the man who has given you more provinces than your ancestors left you cities." Carlos brushed him coldly aside, and though Cortés made repeated efforts to ingratiate himself at court, he died ignored and neglected, in 1547.

Napoleon Bonaparte

It is noteworthy that most conquerors have either not lived to enjoy the fruits of their conquests or have had those fruits turn bitter. Alexander died young, at the height of his glory. Julius Caesar was assassinated. The empires of Charlemagne and Jenghiz Khan began disintegrating almost as soon as they were won. Cortés died in ignoble oblivion. But probably history's most unhappy conqueror was the one who lived long enough to see his empire and his fame turn to ashes while he watched helplessly from afar. This unhappy man was Napoleon Bonaparte and, ironically, his lifelong motto was *Ubicumque felix:* "Happy wherever I am."

So much has been written about Napoleon that it is something of a surprise to realize that his career as France's great leader spanned a period of little more than twenty years. He was anything but an heroic figure, scarcely over five feet tall, with girlish features and an unhealthy yellow complexion. He never learned to spell French words correctly, and always spoke the language with a thick Italian accent. (He was born Napolione Buonoparte on Corsica, an Italian island annexed by France.) During most of his earlier life, he was poor, debt-ridden and insignificant. Once, when he competed for a prize offered by a French literary academy, his essay was judged fifteenth of the sixteen submitted. Even as a young unknown subaltern he arrogantly considered himself an unrecognized aristocrat. Later, as a successful commander, he despised the soldiers who adored him and would give their lives for him; he kept his uniform doused with perfume so he wouldn't have to "smell their sweat." Later still, he divorced a loving and beloved wife to marry a foreign princess, purely for political reasons.

Napoleon graduated from a French military school just at the time of the French Revolution, when the people had thrown off the yoke of their decadent kings and declared France a republic—and were woefully short of heroes. The young artillery officer showed so much military genius in a number of battles that he rose rapidly through the ranks and was made "general of brigade" in 1793, when he was only twenty-four. Three years later, he was commander-in-chief of France's Army of Italy. Within three more years, he fought and defeated the armies of Italy, Austria and Egypt.

In 1799, he returned to France a popular hero, and at a crucial moment. By this time, the republic had lasted for ten years, and had gone through almost that many changes of government, each more inefficient than the last. If it was to survive, the republic needed a strong hand at the helm—and Napoleon was immediately elected First Consul of the Republic. He did effect sweeping reforms in the government and in the judicial system. He guaranteed religious freedom. He made what had been a shambles of a nation into one of the Great Powers of Europe. He went to war again, against a resurgent Austria, and forced that empire to cede to France all the lands west of the Rhine River—thus the map of France was again that of Caesar's Gaul.

In another vote, the French people made Napoleon the First Consul for life, but he wanted more; he wanted to be remembered as another Charlemagne. He persuaded Pope Pius VII to come from Rome to Paris in 1804 and crown him emperor, as Charlemagne had been crowned by Pope Leo. France was ecstatic, but the rest of Europe saw this upstart emperor as a power-mad tyrant to be eliminated. In the west, England blockaded France with its mighty navy, while in the east Russia began to arm and make threatening noises.

Napoleon decided to deal with Russia first. And at the beginning he did seem to be winning. His army forged all the way to the capital city of Moscow in the autumn of 1812. But the Russians, as they fell back before him, had destroyed everything useful to an army. Napoleon found himself sitting triumphantly in a Moscow empty of people and materiel. And that empty victory was to become a resounding defeat. Russian saboteurs set fire to the city, and the French had to move out. Then the cruel Russian winter came down, and the French had to retreat. They found nothing to eat along the way, no shelter, no fodder for their horses, no warm clothing to steal, and soon the retreat became a rout. The waiting Russian cavalry now swept down on this desperate gang that had been an army, and nearly annihilated it.

With France left all but defenseless, the four Allied powers massed together—Britain, Prussia, Austria and Russia—and invaded Napoleon's own country in 1814. Napoleon had no hope of repelling the invasion, but he thought that if he removed himself from the scene, the Allies would not devastate France. He betook himself into exile on the island of Elba, just off the Italian coast, proclaimed it a principality and ostensibly settled down to rule that little pimple of land. As he had hoped, the Allies were satisfied to withdraw from France when the French restored their old monarchy. They brought the brother of the beheaded former king out of hiding and crowned him as Louis XVIII.

But Napoleon, only forty-five years old, was still in his prime and seething with ambition, and the Allies were foolish to think they had got rid of him so easily. Meanwhile, the French were finding King

Louis intolerably dull and colorless after the dashing Napoleon, and France had sunk again to a second-rate power. Under these auspices and less than a year after abdicating, Napoleon slipped away from Elba and returned to France. He was welcomed as a deliverer and in three weeks' time was again the leader and hero of an ecstatic France.

That was probably his time of greatest glory, but it was to be very short. Just one hundred days after taking command, he was again on his way to exile—in the meantime having fought his last battle, against the English and Prussians, and suffered ultimate defeat on the Belgian field of Waterloo. When he abdicated this time, Napoleon tried to flee to the United States, figuring that he would be warmly received by a people grateful to him for having sold them Louisiana at a bargain price. But this time his enemies gave him no choice of place of exile. He and a few loyal retainers were shipped to the remote island of St. Helena, practically in the middle of the Atlantic Ocean, only 45 square miles in extent and populated by fewer than 5,000 people. Here, prohibited even from corresponding with his family, Napoleon passed the remaining six years of his life.

A man standing on the cliffs of St. Helena is a thousand feet above the sea and the sea wind which blows with great force below him. Just so, Napoleon wandered those cliffs in a dead and monotonous calm, now forever apart from the winds of war and conquest and the making of history. He would return to the farmhouse that was his prison and, at dinner, he'd stare stonily at the motto engraved on his table silver and china: *Ubicumque felix*. In 1821, aged fifty-two, he died of cancer—and of boredom and despair and unhappiness.

The Great Warriors

I too shall lie in the dust when I am dead,
but now let me win noble renown.

—Homer

BRIAN BORU

We have already met a number of the legendary warriors of pre-historic and pre-Christian times. About the year 1000 there lived in Ireland a king and hero named Brían mac Cennéidigh (Brian, son of Kennedy), better known as Brian Boru, after the town of Bórime, near which he had his royal residence. As so often in its history, Ireland was a warren of wrangling little kingdoms, and the peerless warrior Brian spent most of his life fighting one after another until he had united the whole country. His rule was sage and just and remarkably "modern"—for example, Brian founded schools and urged his illiterate people to educate themselves, even sending agents to other countries to buy books.

What most histories don't record is that Brian's most implacable enemy—and one he never defeated—was his vicious wife Gormlaith. She had been married twice before, and evidently had made life intolerable for all her husbands, as witness this description: "Gormlaith was the fairest of all women, and gifted, but it was the talk

105

of men that anything she could meddle in she would do ill." She came to hate her third husband because one of the kingdoms Brian absorbed had previously been ruled by her relatives.

So, behind Brian's back, she offered her hand in marriage to *two* Danish Viking chieftains—Brodar, ruler of the Isle of Man, and Sigurd, ruler of the Orkney Islands—or, rather, to whichever one of them would take Ireland from Brian Boru. It is unlikely that, knowing her reputation, either of the Vikings wanted Gormlaith. But they leaped at the prospect of winning Ireland and making it a Danish colony. While they were preparing to invade the country, Gormlaith busied herself in lining up a "fifth column" of her relatives inside Ireland: the clans Malloy of Leinster and Kinsella of Wexford. Thus, when the Danes invaded in 1014, Brian found himself fighting not just foreigners but fellow Irishmen as well. In this battle, which was to be his last, Brian wanted as usual to ride at the front of his forces. But he was seventy-three years old, and was persuaded to direct the action from a tent behind the lines. He directed well, as can be surmised from the record left by one observer. The Danes were mostly fair-haired men, and when they met Brian's axemen and swordsmen, says that record, "the air was filled with flying golden wisps of hair, as it might be chaff flying from the harvesting of an oat field."

Meanwhile, a traitor in Brian's camp told the old king, untruthfully, that his son Morrow had been slain in the battle. Brian emerged from his tent and asked to be shown where Morrow had fallen. As soon as the traitor had led Brian away from his bodyguards, he slew the old man. There also died that day most of the Danes and their allies, including the leaders Sigurd and Brodar (leaving Gormlaith no one to wed; and we don't know what became of her afterward; she is not mentioned again in Irish history). The surviving invaders and insurgents fled, leaving Brian's united Ireland intact. That battle was significant, and not just for Ireland alone, since it broke the Norse power in Ireland forever and thwarted the Danes' hope of using Ireland as the stepping-stone to a continent-wide empire. Without Brian Boru and his brave men, the history of Europe might have been far different from what it is today.

RICHARD THE LION-HEARTED

In the next century, and eastward of the Irish Sea, the first King Richard came to the throne of England in 1189. He saw little of the country he was to rule for ten years. He was concerned with

England chiefly as a source of revenue, and visited that country only twice, for a few months each time (preferring to be off adventuring). He was to render England nearly bankrupt, but his exploits were also to thrill English pride, and make Englishmen admire and cheer him, and call him "Richard the Lion-Hearted." He represented the very "pattern of the fighting man," wrote Winston Churchill. "He loved war as other men love science and poetry, for the excitement of the struggle and the glow of victory."

   Less than a year after his coronation, Richard left England to join the Third Crusade to free the Holy Land (Palestine) from the occupying infidel, the Moslem Sultan Saladin. Most Englishmen would have preferred that their king stay home and mind the store, but a crusade was a sacred enterprise, so the English emptied their pockets to send Richard and his army on their way. En route, Richard conquered Sicily and Cyprus, but was too intent on reaching the Holy Land to claim these islands for England, and they fell into other hands.

   For two years, princes and armies from all over Europe had been besieging Saladin's stronghold, the city of Acre, but they bickered so much among themselves that Saladin had managed to hold out. However, now came Richard—"fighting always in the most dangerous places, striking down the strongest foes"—and within five weeks, Saladin made a conditional surrender. He would not give up the Holy Land, but he would permit Christian pilgrims free access to Jerusalem, the most holy of cities.

Satisfied with that, Richard started home again. But he was captured in Germany, where the emperor held him for a "king's ransom." Once again, the English dug down in their pockets and came up with the money to free their king. Richard returned home just in time to oust his brother John, who had been ruling in his absence and wanted to continue. Richard reaffirmed his own kingship by being crowned a second time. Then he left for France to defend his possessions there—the provinces of Normandy and Aquitaine. He never saw England again, though he continued to tax, borrow, beg and scrounge money from the English for his wars against the French.

His fighting career came to a sad conclusion during a minor fracas with an insignificant French lord. While laying siege to the lord's castle, Richard rode too near the wall and was struck in the shoulder by a crossbow quarrel. Gangrene set in, and Richard knew his end was near. From his deathbed, he set all his affairs in order, declared his brother John to be his heir as King of England, and even sent for the archer who had shot him, pardoned the man and gave him a purseful of money. Richard died, aged forty-two, on April 6, 1199.

ROBERT THE BRUCE

A century later, another hero arose in the isle of Britain, but this time in the north, in Scotland. In 1296, after many years in which the two kingdoms of England and Scotland had dwelt in amity, King Edward I of England deposed the Scottish king and annexed Scotland as a dependency. The Scots naturally wanted their nation to be their own again, and when, in 1309, a young man named Robert the Bruce assassinated the resident English governor, the Scots acclaimed Robert as their king. Edward immediately sent an army into Scotland which, in six decisive battles, defeated Robert's hastily gathered and ill-equipped forces. Robert was himself forced to flee to a small island off the coast. While there he might have accepted his defeat as final, but, according to legend, he watched a small spider trying to weave a web from one of his cabin's roof-beams to another. Six times the spider swung on its fragile thread toward the farther beam, and six times it fell back. Undaunted, the spider tried again . . . and succeeded. Robert the Bruce murmured, "Just so, I have fought the English six times and lost. If I try a seventh time . . . " He returned to Scotland and again made preparations for war.

King Edward I was now dead, and it was his weak and inept son Edward II who was now King of England and who this time led a mighty army north to put down the Scots under Robert the Bruce. The English Army was so numerous—some 25,000 men—and so strung out along the line of march that when Edward and the vanguard reached the battlefield at Bannockburn it took three days for the rest of the force to close up into formation. The English Army was composed of one half armored horsemen and one half longbowmen. (These longbowmen were England's "secret weapon"; their astounding range and accuracy had won every battle they had been employed in.) On his side, Robert the Bruce had only 10,000 foot-soldiers, armed mainly with spears.

But Robert had deployed his force well; with their backs to a heavy wood, the soldiers couldn't retreat no matter what happened —and the English couldn't get behind them. The English cavalry thundered down upon the waiting Scots and "there arose a great and horrible crash from rending lances and dying horses." So intermingled were the Scottish foot-soldiers and the English knights that the English archers to the rear could not loose their volleys without hitting their own men. The English reeled back in retreat —with cowardly King Edward riding harder than any—and the Scots had done what no opponent had ever done before. Mere spearmen, outnumbered more than two to one, had routed an army of cavalry and supposedly invincible archers.

Robert the Bruce and Edward II came to terms, making Scotland an independent nation once again, and Robert its king. Not long after, Robert the Bruce died, but, in a way, he fought one more battle. Following his dying wish, his embalmed heart was placed in a silver casket and given to his old friend and fellow warrior, Sir James Douglas, to be carried to the Holy Land and buried there. On the way, Sir James tarried in Spain to help some other Christians fight a band of Moors. He suffered a mortal wound in the first charge, but stayed in his saddle long enough to detach the silver casket he carried. He flung it ahead of him into the fray, shouting, "As always—forward, brave heart! Douglas will follow thee or die!" He did die, but the battle was won. Afterward the casket was found and returned to Scotland, where the heart was buried with Robert's body in Melrose Abbey.

JOAN OF ARC

A century later, the English fought another brave heart, one which pulsated in the breast of a teenaged girl. She was born Jeannette d'Arc in the village of Domrémy in the French province of Lorraine, about 1412. She has been called *La Pucelle* ("the virgin"), the Maid of Orléans, the Maid of France, and just The Maid. We know her best as Joan of Arc.

Ever since Duke William of Normandy had become William the Conqueror of England, four hundred years before, the realm of England had encompassed not only the island across the Channel but also the province of Normandy on the mainland. As Joan was growing up, English armies were fighting for even larger slices of France, and had enlisted the province of Burgundy as an ally. All France was in turmoil, and its puny, dull-witted King, Charles VII, king in name only, was doing very little to prevent the overthrow of his country.

Serving as stablegirl at the Domrémy inn, young Joan would often exercise the guests' horses by riding them into the nearby woods —and there she saw visions. There came to her the long-dead Saints Margaret and Catherine and the warrior-archangel Michael to mourn the piteous state of poor, wartorn France. During one visit, when Joan was sixteen, Michael gave her the thunderclap word that as commander of the armies she should be the one to free her unhappy country. Joan was terrified, but one does not shrug off the mandate of an archangel. She made her way to the castle of Chinon and sought audience with the king.

One historian has suggested that a teenaged girl, barging into a beleaguered army's headquarters with a tale of being sent by saints would be committed to a mental hospital. Another historian has suggested that Joan was picked out of obscurity and carefully coached for this task; then introduced at court by desperate nobles who wanted a "divinely inspired" hero or heroine to rally their demoralized troops and to jolt their lethargic king into action. However it all came about, it worked. Joan was closeted with King Charles for two hours. He later remarked, wonderingly, that she had discussed state secrets which could only have been imparted to her by supernatural beings.

Charles and his commanders decided to let Joan try her mettle. A suit of white armor was specially tailored for her figure. (We have no reliable description of Joan, but the females of Lorraine are in general built buxom and ample.) She was provided with a squire, two pages and a banner bearing the motto "Jesus Maria." And off she rode, lance couched at her saddle, to take the important city of Orléans away from the occupying English. Joan herself raised the first scaling ladder against the fortified and cannon-bristling wall—and suffered an arrow in her shoulder. But her troops, inspired by The Maid, fought as never before. Orléans was taken and the English were routed.

Led by Joan, the French retook town after town that the invaders had overrun. Joan was twice again wounded, but never left off fighting. Now even her foes, the soldiers of England and Burgundy, began to half-believe in Joan's "divine inspiration"—and their morale and combat ability suffered accordingly. Then, through a combination of Joan's heroism and the cowardice of the French troops in one town, The Maid was captured. The town was under siege by the Burgundians; Joan had led a force out across the town's drawbridge to attack the enemy; the troops behind her had taken fright, turned tail, fled back into the town and drawn up the bridge, leaving her alone and surrounded.

The English and the Burgundians would gladly have executed her on the spot, but they knew this would only make the French resist more fiercely. They decided instead to discredit her "divine inspiration." They hauled her before a Church court (composed entirely of French priests, but all friendly to the English). This prejudiced court convicted her on twelve counts—including "sinful pride," wearing men's clothes, and claiming to obey the will of God instead of the will of the Church. On May 30, 1431, she went to the stake in the market square of Rouen; her last word, as the flames rose about her, was "Jesus!"

Far from aiding the ambitions of the English and Burgundians, the burning of Joan of Arc seemed to put a curse on their campaign. Though the war lasted for two more decades, the English were inexorably beaten back again and again. Their Burgundian allies went over to the French side, and the English finally lost every acre they had held in what is now totally France. England has never since ruled any piece of Continental Europe. Meanwhile, in 1546, a more impartial Church court canceled all the charges against the martyred Maid, and eventually (but not until 1919) the Roman Catholic Church got around to canonizing her as Saint Joan.

PETER THE GREAT

Not all the great warriors have come from western Europe, however. Peter the Great of Russia may never actually have wielded a sword or a musket himself, but he was a warrior nonetheless—and his first enemy was the poverty and backwardness of his own country. When he became Tsar of Russia in 1689, at the age of seventeen, that nation was little more than a wilderness full of barbaric and ignorant people. But the young tsar twice toured Europe— once in the guise of commoner Peter Mikhailov—so he could the more easily study European arts, sciences, customs and civilized ways. He returned to Russia in 1698 determined to civilize and modernize it, by force if necessary.

Force was necessary. Not all his subjects wanted their "Mother Russia" changed. Peter's half sister Sophia led his own palace guard in a rebellion against him. Peter personally supervised the hanging of every man of the guard, and shut up Sophia in a convent for life. Later, another faction of conservative Russians rebelled and tried to depose him in favor of his teenaged son Alexis. The revolutionaries were deported to the lead mines of Siberia, and Alexis was beaten to death in his jail cell.

Peter's improvements in Russia ranged from the ruthless to the ridiculous. With his own hand, he shaved the heavy beards (time-honored symbols of mature wisdom) from every man of his court so they'd resemble clean-shaven European courtiers. Policemen with scissors patrolled every country road, shearing the locks of passing peasants. But Peter also amassed an army of 200,000 men and Russia's first rudimentary navy: some fifty ships, built by imported European shipwrights. He laid out roads, built towns, created industries, dug canals and mines, founded schools and universities and hospitals. He established Russia's first printing shops, which printed Russia's first books.

Peter looked abroad as well, and he knew that for Russia to develop fully, it must have access to the open seas, which it then did not. Tsar Peter (as "Captain Peter Aleksyeevich") personally led his newly-built naval fleet in an assault on the Turkish fortress port of Azov, conquered it, and thus had an outlet to the Black Sea and the Mediterranean. Next he looked to the Baltic Sea in the north, but in those days mighty Sweden controlled the whole north of Europe. Peter led his big but unwieldy and ill-trained army into battle against the Swedes—and was most disastrously defeated.

The Swedes' young king, Charles XII, was emboldened by that victory to go on a rampage through Europe, sacking Poland, Saxony, and Denmark. While Charles was thus engaged, Tsar Peter took the opportunity to drill and train his army with demonic energy. By the time the Swedish troops turned back toward Sweden, tired now and somewhat depleted, Peter was ready and waiting for them—and practically wiped them out. In the resulting peace treaty, Sweden ceded all her Baltic provinces to Russia—and Peter now had a long, open coastline along the Baltic Sea. Russia had replaced Sweden as the leading power of northern Europe.

It has been written of Peter that "all his qualities were on a colossal scale. His rage was cyclonic: his hatred rarely stopped short of extermination. His banquets were orgies. He lived and he loved like

one of the giants of old." He was also subject to frequent and agonizing convulsive fits, and from one of them he died in 1725. But
it was also said of Peter the Great that "he never destroyed anything which he was not able to replace by something better."
Though he made many enemies in destroying Old Russia, most
people regarded him as a hero for having brought a New Russia
into the modern world. Although it later fell on bad times, Russia
has never relinquished what it gained from Peter's reign.

FREDERICK THE GREAT

The next "Great" in our roll call of warriors is Frederick the
Great, who made his domain of Prussia the largest and most important of the states of Germany. He was born in 1712 and for most
of his early years seemed destined for anything but greatness. His
father, King Frederick William I, was a harsh old soldier who tried
to bring up Frederick in his warlike ways, but the boy contrarily
developed a taste for literature and music, refused to ride or shoot,
preferred the French language and dress, and showed open con-
tempt for German customs. Once, in company with a friend, Frederick tried to escape from his demanding father and flee to France.
The two runaways were caught, and the king forced Frederick to
watch while his young friend was beheaded.

Years later, one of Frederick's advisers happened to remark that
"the inborn inclination of men is rather to good than to evil." Frederick made the melancholy reply, "Ah, my dear Sulzer, you don't
know this damned human race." Once he attained the throne,
though—whatever he thought of the human race—Frederick did his
best to be a good and fair ruler. He became king in 1740 and immediately repealed most of his father's stern laws. He abolished
torture, for example, and instituted religious freedom. He set up
a Chamber of Justice at Berlin which was empowered to overrule
even himself, the king, should he err in dispensing justice.

He had been king for only two years when he led his army in
his first battle, against the Austrians, and earned his first reputation—a reputation for cowardice—when his troops saw him galloping madly away from the battlefield. But that was not his fault;
he had been told mistakenly that his men were defeated, and thought
he was leading a retreat. In fact, his Prussians had won the day.
And they kept on winning battles—directed by Frederick's military
genius, which no one could deny—for the next fourteen years. Fi-

nally Prussia became so powerful that practically all the rest of Europe—Austria, France, Russia, Sweden and Saxony—ganged up together to erase the Prussian menace.

In this Seven Years' War (1756–63), the Prussians fought unaided against the five allied countries. In this war, Frederick—who, at the head of his armies, usually rode unhesitatingly into shot and shell—not only proved himself no coward but he also won the unequal contest. There is no need to detail the countless marches and maneuvers of this long war. It is sufficient to say that Frederick distinguished himself personally by leading many a battle, siege and skirmish, and brilliantly directed his other generals and their separate forces. The books he later wrote on wartime strategy and tactics became textbooks for generations of military men.

By the end of the war, Prussia was conceded to be one of the Great Powers of the Continent, and Frederick was hailed by his own people as the "Great." He lived to the ripe old age of seventy-two, and might have lived longer, but he insisted on reviewing a parade of his troops, sitting stoically on his horse through several hours of pouring rain. He caught a cold, which worsened to pneumonia, and he died on August 17, 1786. He was buried, as he had commanded, beside the graves of the two best-loved companions of his old age—not members of "this damned human race," but his two faithful greyhounds.

Horatio Nelson

The greatest of England's army and naval heroes were born just eleven years apart, and did much of their fighting during the same era. One on land, one on sea, they accomplished many separate victories and both were involved in the defeat of Napoleon.

In 1770, a twelve-year-old went to sea as a cabin boy in the Royal Navy. Four years later, by which time he had sailed from the Arctic to the East Indies and was an able seaman, he had seen no action and was depressed by the belief that he was growing old without yet making a name for himself. This would seem silly in a teenager, except that he be Horatio Nelson. The young lad decided at the age of sixteen, as we know from a memoir he wrote long afterward when he was the famous Admiral Lord Nelson, "I *will* be a hero, and, confiding in Providence, I will brave every danger."

He was a full captain at twenty—"the merest boy of a captain

I ever beheld," remarked the King of England, who met him at that time. "There was something irresistibly pleasing in his conversation, and an enthusiasm, that showed he was no common being." Nelson's charm was his greatest asset; it endeared him to his superiors, to his subordinate officers, and to his lowest-ranking sailors; there was never a man who served with him but wouldn't have fought his best for Nelson. Nelson's faculty of commanding loving obedience, combined with his own genius and courage in combat, made him and his "band of brothers" (as he called his men) the most successful and renowned warriors in the history of the Royal Navy.

Fighting the French during their Revolutionary Wars, Nelson helped capture Corsica—and received a wound that cost him the sight of one eye. Later, fighting the Spanish, he ignored the timid orders coming from London, and defeated the Spanish fleet off Cape St. Vincent. Soon after, Nelson led the unsuccessful English attempt to take Santa Cruz de Tenerife, this time losing his right arm. During the months of inaction while he recovered from the crude amputation, Napoleon Bonaparte took command of the French forces. Napoleon led his army to Egypt and had just conquered the country when Nelson's squadron came sailing offshore and destroyed the French fleet there, stranding Napoleon and his whole army in Egypt, and making that conquest a rather hollow victory for him. Napoleon had to make his way back without his army (though he soon assembled another). Meanwhile, Nelson made his headquarters in Naples, in the Kingdom of the Two Sicilies, and here he indulged in a glaringly scandalous love affair with the stunningly beautiful Lady Emma Hamilton, wife of the English ambassador. It confirms Nelson's reputation for charm that a man with only one arm and one eye should be able to captivate one of the most beautiful women of his time.

Next, Nelson was assigned to the Baltic Sea, where an English fleet was blockading the Denmark port of Copenhagen. When the blockade became a battle, the fleet's commander-in-chief ran up signal flags on his ship ordering Nelson and his squadron to retire from action. Nelson coolly put his telescope to his blind eye, said, "I see no signals," and went on fighting—totally defeating the Danes. The French and Spanish now combined their navies, hoping by sheer bulk to end the British rule of the seas. But Nelson sailed against their combined flotilla, encountering it off Cape Trafalgar on the coast of Spain in October, 1805. Though the French-Spanish fleet outnumbered his, and had the benefit of a friendly port near by, Nelson forced the enemy ships into open waters where they had to fight. He then fought them to a finish, destroying or capturing 60 per cent of their combined fleet. "Trafalgar is regarded as the greatest of naval battles," wrote a historian a century later, "and Nelson as the greatest of admirals."

Unfortunately, just at the moment of victory, Nelson suffered his last and mortal wound, shot in the spine by a sniper aboard a French ship. His last words were, "Thank God I have done my duty." The great admiral's body, doubled-up in a cask of rum to preserve it, was brought back to England in his flagship, the *Victory*, for a hero's funeral. The carriage which bore his coffin in the procession was a small-scale model of the *Victory*, and the coffin itself was carved from the mainmast of one of the French warships he had vanquished.

THE DUKE OF WELLINGTON

In 1787, an eighteen-year-old, fresh out of military school, joined the British Army as an ensign. At the age of twenty-four he was lieutenant-colonel of his regiment, but—like Horatio Nelson at sixteen—he was annoyed at having yet seen no action. Very shortly after, however, this young man, Arthur Wellesley, was to start his rise which, on land, matched that of Nelson's at sea. In 1796, he was sent to England's colony of India, and there he put down one rebellion after another among the insurgent maharajahs—at one time defeating an army of 40,000 rebels with only 10,000 men of his own. So spectacular were his victories in India that when he returned to England in 1805, he was knighted and easily elected to Parliament. But he was disinclined to settle into political life just yet; two years later he was leading an expedition against the still-unconquered Danes.

Then he invaded Spain—an invasion made possible because, after Nelson's victory at Trafalgar, there was no enemy war fleet to impede his landing—and expelled Napoleon's forces from that country. He went on into southern France, and it was partly this invasion which persuaded Napoleon to exile himself on the island of Elba. For these feats, Wellesley was created Duke of Wellington. He was forever thereafter called "the Iron Duke" by his soldiers, by the admiring populace of England, and by the numerous enemies who had felt his might—for Wellington was no charmer like Nelson; he accomplished his victories by force of cold will and unbending discipline.

When Napoleon suddenly returned from Elba for his final "hundred days" try for a comeback, Wellington was put in command of all the Allied armies. At Waterloo, Wellington and his generals decisively defeated Napoleon and drove him into the exile from which he never returned. During the next three disorganized years, Wellington practically governed France, holding it together until a stable government could be established.

Wellington was almost as astute a statesman as he was warrior. He went on many diplomatic missions to foreign countries as an emissary of his government. For the two-year period of 1828 to 1830 he was premier of England as Prime Minister. Until nearly the age of eighty, the Iron Duke remained commander-in-chief of the British Army, and also continued to serve in one parliamentary office or another. Unlike so many other great warriors, he died peacefully in bed, in 1852, and was buried (near Lord Nelson) under the dome of St. Paul's Cathedral, in a coffin of bronze melted down from the cannons he had captured from Napoleon at Waterloo.

GEORGE WASHINGTON

The United States had many a hero before the country became the United States—Nathaniel Bacon, John Peter Zenger, Daniel Boone and others, but the American Revolution naturally produced the earliest great warriors of the United States. "First in war" and foremost among them, of course, was George Washington. By 1775, when "the shot heard round the world" started the Revolution, Washington had retired from military service and was a prosperous Virginia planter. He was just forty-three years old, and was in his prime, standing six feet three inches and weighing more than two hundred pounds. He was an accomplished horseman, an experienced military officer, and patriotically dedicated to the colonies' independence. Thus, he was the natural choice to lead the thirteen colonies' separate militia troops combined into a "Continental Army." Washington insisted he was not worthy of the honor, but he accepted the commission on condition that he be paid nothing but his expenses. That was just as well, because the Continental Congress had practically no money to pay for anything—and it didn't provide Washington with much of an army, either.

He never had more than 20,000 men altogether, even when, late in the war, France sent troops to help. The Continentals were raw volunteers from civilian life, barely trained, unused to discipline, ill-fed, ill-clothed, ill-equipped, seldom paid, and sometimes even barefoot. The men from different colonies squabbled among themselves and often refused to aid each other when hard-pressed in battle. During one crucial confrontation with the British in New York City, the entire Connecticut force fled in a mass panic of cowardice. But the other contingents were little better. When Washington led a retreat from the city and across New Jersey, much of his army melted away behind him, the men simply wandering off toward their homes.

Washington is rightly remembered as a great fighting general—though actually he lost about as many battles as he won. His chief claim to heroism lay in his ability to hold that army together, particularly in such dark days as the bitter winter at Valley Forge, Pennsylvania, when his men nearly starved and froze to death. Always, it seemed, when the whole army was about to desert in a body, Washington would somehow force a battle with the British—and win it. This would put new vigor into his troops, bring other patriots flocking to join him, and keep the thirteen colonies from simply abandoning their Revolution in apathy and discouragement.

Though other generals and other brave men (including foreigners who came to help the cause) did their part in effecting the final victory, Washington was indisputably the warrior who did most to win the colonies' independence. "First in peace"—he was a prime mover in welding the disparate colonies into the United States, and in framing the Constitution that still directs the nation's destiny. (While campaigning for the Constitution's adoption, Washington wrote: "It or dis-union is before us to chuse from." He never could spell.) "First in the hearts of his countrymen," he was inevitably the choice for the new nation's first President.

Washington could have been President for life (indeed, there were several people who wanted to crown him King), but he refused a third term, thus setting a precedent that is now law: no President may serve more than two terms. He went back to his Virginia plantation and settled down to be a gentleman-farmer once more. In 1799, at the age of sixty-seven, he spent too long a day in the saddle, on a day of rain and sleet, and—like Frederick the Great—caught a fatal ailment. When news of his death reached Europe, even his old opponents, the British, mourned his passing. Their Channel fleet of warships fired a cannon salute, and that was answered by *their* enemies, the armies of the French, whose cannon echoed the salute to the late great warrior.

John Paul Jones

While Washington was fighting the Revolution on land, its greatest naval hero was "founding the American naval tradition." It is a bit difficult to think of him as an American, however, because in his short life he spent no more than six or seven years ashore in the United States. He was born John Paul in Scotland, and ran away to sea at the age of twelve. It is known that he served for several years on slave ships until he quit that trade in disgust, and it is rumored that he also served for a time on a pirate ship.

However that may be, he showed up in Philadelphia at the beginning of the Revolution, offering his services and calling himself John Paul Jones. In 1776, he was given a captain's commission, a small warship and orders to free-lance—that is, to sail where and when he thought best "for distressing the enemies of the United States." In his first seven weeks at sea, he sank eight British craft and captured eight more.

Then Jones was sent to France, where a splendid new battle frigate was supposedly waiting for him. But the French—at that time not at war with Great Britain—feared to risk British displeasure, and refused to hand over the ship. Jones was stranded in France, supporting himself and his crew out of his own pocket for several months. Finally, with the help of Benjamin Franklin, then the United States' emissary to France, Jones acquired an old merchant ship. He converted the clumsy vessel, as best he could, into a fighting ship and named it the *Bon Homme Richard* (in honor of Franklin, author of *Poor Richard's Almanack*).

Jones put to sea in this creaky old tub and immediately sailed into one of the most famous sea battles of all time. He encountered a fleet of British merchantmen, convoyed by the heavily-armed, speedy and deadly warship *Serapis*. The *Bon Homme Richard* closed with her at sunset; the battle was concluded by moonlight. At one point, Jones' guns had set twelve separate fires aboard the *Serapis*, but the guns of the *Serapis* had holed the *Bon Homme Richard* at the waterline, and she was settling lower and lower into the sea. Jones boldly threw grapples across the space between the two ships, lashed his ship to the side of the *Serapis*, and his men battled across the gunwales with muskets, swords and pikes.

The English captain called for his surrender—and fully expected it. But Jones shouted back the classic reply, "Sir, I have not yet begun to fight!" And in the end it was the English captain who surrendered. Jones and his men clambered aboard the *Serapis* and took possession—just in time, too, for by morning the *Bon Homme Richard* had sunk.

That was John Paul Jones' last conquest for the United States. He sailed the *Serapis* to France, hoping to patch her up and take her to sea as his own warship. But political delays kept Jones ashore and the *Serapis* in drydock until the Revolution was over. Jones did not return to the United States until 1787, when he was given a gold medal (and something of a brush-off) by Congress.

Still itching for sea duty, Jones accepted an offer from Russia's Tsarina Catherine the Great to come and put some fire into Russia's rather fusty navy. He did, and served with distinction in Russia's longstanding war with the Turks. But he fell out of favor with Catherine and, broken in health and spirit, retired to Paris, where, just forty-five years old, he died. Never properly honored in his lifetime, John Paul Jones was forgotten in death. Even his gravesite was unknown until, a hundred years later, an American ambassador searched for and found it. The hero's remains were ceremoniously brought back across the Atlantic by a fleet of American warships. In 1913, John Paul Jones was properly interred in the chapel of the U.S. Naval Academy at Annapolis, Maryland.

THADDEUS KOSCIUSKO

Many foreign champions of liberty joined the United States in their fight for independence. Among them was a young Pole, Tadeusz Kościuszko (later anglicized as Thaddeus Kosciusko). He had studied at military schools all over Europe, but found no use for his talents in his native Poland, then a mere and miserable dependency of the great powers of Russia and Prussia. Unable to help his own nation, Kosciusko came to help free the American colonies. General Washington made him his personal adjutant and even though he was a foreigner and a high officer, Kosciusko was much loved by the officers and troops of the Continental Army. He held West Point against the British, helped defeat them in New York, fought with distinction in the Carolinas, and helped force the British into their final surrender at Yorktown, Virginia.

After the war a grateful Congress heaped honors on him: American citizenship, an annual pension, a large estate, and the rank of brigadier general. Kosciusko enjoyed these bounties only briefly, however, for in 1791 his homeland of Poland began stirring toward independence under a new constitution. Kosciusko hurried home to help, but he was less successful in freeing Poland than he had been in America. Throughout their history, the Poles have been ground under the heel either of their own not-very-noble nobility or of a foreign power. Kosciusko hoped to win Poland's recognition as a nation as well as end the class divisions which kept the mass of Poles ignorant, poverty-stricken and practically slaves.

For a time, it appeared that he might just do that—he defeated the Russian armies in three pitched battles—but the Polish nobles, anxious to keep their ancient privileges, withdrew their troops from the conflict. Kosciusko, left with only a small, weak army of peasants, held off the Russians for a time. But then the inevitable happened. Both Austria and Prussia moved against him and, in 1794, his pitiful little army was almost annihilated. Kosciusko himself was seriously wounded and taken prisoner. Austria, Prussia and Russia divided up his country, and the name of Poland disappeared from the map, not to reappear for more than a hundred years.

Kosciusko spent the remainder of his life traveling—to Philadelphia (then the U.S. capital), Paris, Vienna—pleading always for support for his vanished Poland, but without success. Old, worn out, discouraged, he died in Switzerland in 1817. Poland was not re-established as an independent nation until 1918, after the First World War. It was overrun by Nazi Germany in the Second World War and afterward became a satellite of the Soviet Union. However, despite Poland's dreary record of one subjugation after another, Kosciusko is still revered by Poles as a great warrior and hero.

Robert E. Lee

The American Civil War provided heroes aplenty from both the "Yankee" United States and the "Rebel" Confederate states. It is curious, though, that the best-remembered warrior in that war should be the general who turned his back on the Union he had heroically served for many years, and then did his best to defeat it. Even in the Northern states, to this day, Confederate General Robert E. Lee is more admired than any Union officer—even including General Ulysses S. Grant, who won the war and later became President.

Robert Edward Lee was born in Virginia, son of Henry ("Light-

Horse Harry") Lee, a hero of the American Revolution. He graduated from the U.S. Military Academy at West Point and served with distinction as a U.S. Army officer in the Mexican War and in many skirmishes with the Indians. Still Robert E. Lee thought of himself not as an "American" but as a "Virginian." In 1861, on the eve of the Civil War, he was called to Washington and offered supreme command of the Union forces. Had he accepted, the war would doubtless have ended much sooner, and with less death, devastation and bitterness on both sides. But Lee replied to the offer by saying, "If the Union is dissolved, I shall return to my native state and share the miseries of my people and, save in defense, will draw my sword no more."

When Virginia seceded, Lee resigned his U.S. Army commission and became military adviser to Confederate President Jefferson Davis. In truth, Lee did not fight—except for one brief and unsuccessful campaign against the Yankees in western Virginia—until the war was a year old. The first commander of the Rebel forces in Virginia was General Joseph E. Johnston, and it was not until Johnston was wounded at Fair Oaks in May, 1862, that Lee took command of the Army of Northern Virginia. (The foremost Yankee hero of the war, General Grant, did not become commander-in-chief of the Union forces until 1864, just a year before the war ended.)

Undeniably a military genius, Lee might well have won the war for the Confederacy, except that he was handicapped by a scarcity of troops, arms, ammunition and supplies. The Northern states had more men, more manufacturing facilities, and a navy which effectually blocked all the Southern ports from receiving badly needed supplies from sympathetic England and France. The war lasted as long as it did partly because so many of the Union generals were absolute bunglers who couldn't defeat the Rebels in battles where the Yankees outnumbered them four to one, and partly because Lee was such a superb general that he could do wonders with much fewer men and guns.

The turning point of the war came when Lee's Army of Northern Virginia made its second Northern invasion in June of 1863 and met a better equipped and strongly entrenched Union army at Gettysburg, Pennsylvania. The battle lasted for three days and cost the lives of nearly 45,000 men. When Lee pulled back—ironically, on the Fourth of July—it was obvious that the Confederacy's defeat was only a matter of time.

Mainly thanks to General Grant, the Yankees held the whole Mississippi River, thus splitting the Confederacy from north to south. Within another year, the Union General William T. Sherman had taken Atlanta, Georgia, and then made his famous "march to the sea," cutting the Confederacy from west to east. In the last days, Lee was defending the Confederate capital of Richmond, Virginia, and this static defense deprived him of his most useful weapon, mobility. In one last gamble, he abandoned Richmond and made a desperate march to unite with Johnston's army in North Carolina. He didn't make it; Grant overtook him at the little hamlet of Appomattox Courthouse; there, on April 2, 1865, Lee handed over his sword in unconditional surrender. He asked only that his men be allowed to keep their horses and mules "for their spring plowing"—and Grant graciously agreed.

Lee mounted his own dapple-gray horse "Traveler" and rode home, never to take up arms again. He accepted the post of president of Washington College in Lexington, Virginia (later renamed Washington and Lee University) and spent his last years—he died in 1870—teaching the precepts of peace and harmony in a united nation, and inspiring his students to be not just good Virginians but good Americans.

I have my own favorite wartime warrior, though I never knew him to slay a single enemy or win a single medal. I came upon him unexpectedly in a little village on a remote island in the China Sea, a place where I was surprised to find another white man, this one wearing a cassock and Roman collar. He was a missionary Catholic priest, redheaded, wreathed with smiles, speaking both English and the native language with a heavy Irish brogue.

This was during the Korean War, and the island's mountains were full of enemy guerrillas, but some of the priest's Korean flock lived in those mountains, and nothing would deter him from visiting them on a crippled old horse, the only vehicle available to him. This was a war fought with bullets, bombs, rockets and napalm, yet the only defensive weapon that brave and jolly priest carried with him into those perilous mountains was a homemade bow and arrows. I'm afraid I have long forgotten the dear man's name, and I have no idea what became of him after I left that island. But whenever I think of him, fondly and admiringly, I think of Friar Tuck.

The Great Adventurers

They set their course by God and by guess. If luck was
with them they returned after one or two or three
years. In the other case, their bleached bones remained
behind. But they were true pioneers. They gambled
with luck. Life to them was a glorious adventure.
—Hendrik Willem van Loon

MARCO POLO

Marco Polo's twenty-four years of wandering around Asia certainly
should make him the beau ideal of an adventurer. He was only
about seventeen when he left his native Venice in 1271, to travel
with his father Niccolo and Uncle Maffeo to foreign lands. They
were hardheaded businessmen, and made a handsome profit from
their travels, but Marco was also a curious and keen-eyed observer.
He noted everything of interest and seemingly never forgot a thing.

The Polos were not the first westerners to venture into China. For
ages there had been a western trade with China—even the pharaohs
of ancient Egypt had worn Chinese silk—but by this time most of
that trade was carried on by sea, by Arab merchants. The Polos were
the first men in centuries to make the long trek overland; also, they
were the first to venture into certain corners of Asia which were not
again to be seen by white men until almost the turn of our present
century. And, as an added accomplishment, Marco was the first to

leave a mainly accurate account of the marvels of the Orient.

More than three years after leaving Venice, the Polos arrived at the Chinese city of Campuluc (immortalized by the poet Coleridge as "Xanadu," and now known as Peking), the capital of Kublai Khan, great-great-great-grandson of Jenghiz Khan. The Khan received them warmly, entertained them royally, and soon developed a considerable affection for them. He let them wander at will throughout his lands and into others, from the Gobi Desert to the Burma jungles, and even appointed Marco (who had learned the language) governor of the city of Kiangtu for three years.

The Polos had all manner of adventures. For a long time, the Khan had been trying to conquer a city called Sa-yan-fu. It was on an island in a lake, and was well-stocked with food and supplies. So it was impossible to take by siege or to starve into submission. Niccolo and Maffeo Polo designed, and the Khan's artisans built, catapults which threw 300-pound boulders across the water into the city—and Sa-yan-fu soon surrendered. Meanwhile, Marco continued finding wonders and oddities. He marveled that the Chinese used paper money, at that time unknown in Europe. (It was black, and bore the handwritten signatures of numerous officials and the red seal of the Khan.) He visited Ziamba (Siam) and what he found most noteworthy there was that "the king had three hundred and twenty-six children." Marco stood on the shore of the China Sea (an extension of the Pacific) and remarked—one of his few mistaken assumptions —that, though called "the Sea of Chin," it of course had to be the Atlantic Ocean.

Rich from eighteen years of trading throughout Asia, Niccolo, Maffeo and Marco were ready to depart. The Khan provided them with a ship, on the condition that they would deliver a royal maiden named Kukachin to marry a grandnephew of his in Persia. The four, with a sturdy crew and plenty of servants, set sail from Changchow in 1292. They were delayed several times en route, sometimes by the need to restock the ship, sometimes merely by Marco's curiosity. For instance, he took time to discover, somewhere on the Java coast, the intriguing fact that the people there worshipped not gods but all kinds of objects, "for each person adores throughout the day the first thing he sees when he awakes in the morning."

It took them two years to get as far as Persia and deliver the Lady Kukachin, and another year to get home to Venice. (Besides silks, spices, jewels and other treasures, they brought a Chinese curiosity of cookery, which the Venetians called *spaghetti*.)

Some of the wonders Marco reported on his return were so incredible that his fellow Venetians considered him a swaggering fraud, and nicknamed him "Marco of the Millions" (of lies). For example, who could possbly believe that one of the Himalaya Mountains produced a fiber from its rocks which the natives spun into thread and wove into a cloth that was fireproof? (It was, of course, asbestos.) Marco did not confine his observations to the marvelous, but also reported candidly on the peoples he encountered. On Armenia: "In former times its people were expert and brave soldiers, but now they are great drinkers, cowardly and worthless." On the inhabitants of what is now the southernmost portion of the Soviet Union: "They are a rude people and dull of intellect." On the Bactrians of what is now Afghanistan: "They are a handsome race, especially the women, who, in my opinion, are the most beautiful in the world."

Marco might never have written the marvelous narrative of his adventures, except that in 1298 he chanced to get embroiled in a petty war between the city-states of Genoa and Venice, and was confined in a Genoa jail for nearly a year. His cellmate happened to be a writer, and Marco entertained him with his tales of adventure. The writer set them all down. The narrative was published with the somewhat immodest title of *A Description of the World*. Even in writing, Marco's stories were still not believed. When he was on his deathbed at the age of seventy, in 1324, his family and friends beseeched him to renounce all his hoaxes and humbug so his soul wouldn't be damned. Marco's last words were that he had no lies to renounce, that in fact he had told only about half of his wondrous adventures.

CHRISTOPHER COLUMBUS

More than a century after Polo's death, Christopher Columbus carried on his 1492 voyage a well-thumbed copy of *A Description of the World*. He actually used Marco Polo's narrative as a basis for his navigational calculations, which he expected would lead him from Spain westward across the Atlantic to Japan.

Though Columbus (as we call him) sailed under the flag of Spain (where he was called Cristóbal Colón), he was born Cristoforo Colombo in Genoa, the city that had once jailed Marco Polo of Venice. He spent years of frustration in trying to convince some patron that he could reach Japan, China and India by sailing west across the Atlantic—and in trying to get some patron to finance just such voyage. Finally Ferdinand and Isabella, king and queen of Spain, paid for the ships, men and supplies.

It has been well established that Columbus was not the discoverer of America. The very first to discover it were, of course, the "Indians" who came across the land bridge between Asia and Alaska countless eons ago. Nor was Columbus the first *white* discoverer of America. The Vikings had found it some five hundred years before him, and even had a colony for a while in Newfoundland and perhaps another in Massachusetts or thereabouts. There is some evidence that Asian mariners may also, either deliberately or wind-driven, have sailed all the way east across the Pacific and made contact with the natives of western Central and South America.

This is not to detract from Columbus' achievement. It *was* heroic of Columbus to venture out into what was then the Unknown. Despite the fact that others had discovered the New World before him, and despite the fact that Columbus believed to his dying day (after making four voyages) that he was visiting "the Indies" every time,

still he deserves credit for opening up the New World to colonization and the making use of its treasures and resources. He was most
disappointed, and himself denounced Polo as a fraud, when he landed (so he thought) far south of Japan, in some islands off India. Of
course we know that his landfall was in the Bahamas off North
America, and that the "Indians" he met there were really Lucayos,
a tribe of gentle indigenes.

Not only did Columbus never realize he had discovered a whole
new continent but, unsuspected by the civilized world, he was not
the first of his crew to set foot on it. Let us pause here to record one
of the most thoroughly forgotten "firsts" in history. When Columbus'
crew let down their longboat from the ship *Santa Maria,* and rowed
Columbus ashore, the boat scraped bottom several yards from the
dry beach. One of the crew jumped into the surf to lighten the boat
and drag it to the sand. That "first white man to touch the New
World" was—and you can win bets on this—an Irishman named
Patrick McGuire.

Incidentally, Columbus' expedition wreaked another vengeance
on Venice. Ever since Polo's epic trek, Venice had been the starting
point for overland trade with the Orient, and the Venetian street
of bankers and stockbrokers, called the Rialto, had become the "Wall
Street" of Europe. When the news came that Columbus had sailed
to "India" in little more than two months, it was evident to everybody that the long and tedious overland haul from Venice was no
longer necessary. Everybody was in error, but the Rialto went into
a panic, stocks and bonds plummeted in value, and any number of
people all over Europe were bankrupted.

Even if Columbus hadn't found America when he did, it would
have been discovered anyway, just eight years later, by another
European who wasn't looking for it and didn't even want to be
there. The man was Pedro Alvares Cabral, and he was commander
of a Portuguese fleet making the routine trade run around Africa
toward the Orient. In 1500, his flotilla ran into a storm, was blown off
course far to the west, and he found himself sailing along the coast
of Brazil.

FERDINAND MAGELLAN

Another mariner, who did know where he was headed, has never
gotten better than second billing to Columbus in the history books,
though his voyage was really much riskier and more heroic. He was

Ferdinand Magellan, a Portuguese captain in the employ of Spain, who sailed with five ships from Seville in 1519. Besides Magellan, who never returned, at least eighteen of his men deserve equal commemoration as heroes. Of the 265 officers and sailors who left Seville that day, these eighteen were the only ones who completed the voyage and lived to see Spain again, three years later.

Magellan sailed south to Africa, then followed Alvares Cabral's course across the Atlantic to Brazil, thence southward along the coast of South America. It was no pleasure cruise, however. When nine Spaniards rowed a boat ashore at an inviting river, to lay-on fruits and fresh water, they were seized by cannibal natives, butchered alive and eaten raw. The fleet came at last to the "tail" of South America, and sailed around it through the narrow passage between two cliffs which is still called the Strait of Magellan. It has been called worse things. A much later captain, in a sturdy iron ship, said, "There is not in the world a coast more terrible than this!" The waves there break on the enclosing ice-covered cliff walls with a roar that can be heard twenty miles inland.

Magellan's little cockleshell craft took five weeks to fight their way through the boiling seas and blizzard winds of that passage, which is only 330 miles long. The captain of Magellan's biggest vessel simply gave up and sailed back for Spain. The smallest vessel broke apart and sank. On still another ship, four men tried to lead the rest of the crew in mutiny, Magellan had two of the mutineers executed and the other two marooned on that fearsome shore, a fate crueler than instant death.

The remaining three ships emerged at last from the infernal strait into a vast ocean that seemed placid and serene by comparison. Magellan named it *Mare Pacífico,* "the Peaceful Sea." Then, for ninety-eight days they sailed ever westward without a sight of land where they might provision. The mariners suffered terribly from hunger and thirst. They ate the rats that infested the ships, and when there were no more rats, they chewed pieces of sailcloth, hoping that this pretense of eating would quell their ravenous hunger. Nineteen men died during that time.

In March of 1521, they finally sighted an island (perhaps today's Guam) and were able to restock the ships' galleys. But while they worked the island, the natives stole all the sailors' possessions they could lay hands on. Hence Magellan named the islands of that group the *Ladrones* ("thieves"). Their next landfall was another cluster of islands, which Magellan dubbed the *Filipinas,* after the young Crown

Prince Felipe of Spain. Here they were well received by the two rulers—King Five-Wives and King Kolambu—of an island named Cebú, and even converted more than a thousand of the Cebuanos to Christianity.

Magellan and his men agreed to help the Cebuanos punish an enemy tribe on another island. In the ensuing battle, despite their superior weapons, the Spaniards were routed. Magellan took a poisoned arrow in his right leg and a slash across the face. When he fell, the natives literally minced him with their own bamboo spears and with metal cutlasses taken from his men. The survivors of the battle ran for their ships, but there were no longer enough men to crew all three; they hastily burned one ship and fled in the other two.

During the remainder of their voyage, they discovered other unknown lands, including the Moluccas (the long-sought, almost legendary "Spice Islands"), Borneo and Timor. One of the two ships began to leak and to fall behind, but they were in trade waters, and its crew was picked up by a passing Portuguese merchantman. The one remaining ship, the *Vittoria,* plowed on. The crew narrowly missing sighting Australia (not to be discovered for another two hundred years), crossed the Indian Ocean, rounded Africa and finally reached Spain. By now it bore a skeleton crew of seventeen men and one officer, Sebastián del Cano, who received from King Carlos V, with great ceremony, the right to bear forever a family coat-of-arms inscribed *Primus circumdedisti me* ("I was the first around the world").

HENRY HUDSON

For a hundred years Spain and Portugal practically ruled the southern seas and the sea routes to both the New World and the Orient—and jealously guarded them from use by any other nation's ships—so the mariners of northern countries began venturing farther and farther across their northern seas. They had one fixed belief: that the route around Africa to the Orient could not be the only one, that there had to be another way through the northern latitudes of the world. For centuries they sought, alternately, a "Northeast Passage": trying to sail around the northern rim of Russia; and a "Northwest Passage": trying to sail around the northern rim of America—but forever finding both routes blocked by impassable ice and a cold too terrible to bear.

That search led one of the bravest of English seafarers, Henry Hudson, to a tragic end. After making several voyages seeking a Northeast Passage, sometimes for England, sometimes for the Dutch, and every time being balked by the Arctic ice, Hudson finally gave up and, in 1609, went looking for a Northwest Passage instead. His plan was to sail northward along the Atlantic coast of North America, investigating every big river to see if it flowed all the way from the Pacific. This is, to us, a ludicrous notion, but in those days nobody knew how immensely wide North America really is.

Hudson started by sailing up Virginia's Chesapeake Bay, suggested to him as a "possible" passage by his friend and fellow explorer, Captain John Smith, who had founded the Jamestown Colony near by. As he sailed along it, the wide bay dwindled into the numerous rather puny rivers which feed it—so Hudson turned back to sea and went north. He came to what is now the Bay of New York, outlet of the river which now bears his name, and this one really looked promising. At that time, great whales swam upriver as far as where Albany now stands. And that's how far Hudson got, before he decided that the river, running almost due north, was never going to bend westward toward the Pacific. He returned to Europe, but the voyage had not been wasted. He was sailing for the Dutch at that time, and this voyage gave them their first claim on "Nieuw Amsterdam."

In 1610, Hudson was back again, this time in the little ship *Discovery,* flying the British flag and determined to try the much higher latitudes. He sailed well north of Labrador, through the narrows now called Hudson Strait, and turned southwest into the vast inland sea now called Hudson Bay. Had he steered northwest instead, he would have found the passage he sought, but his flimsy sailing ship could never have got through. It was not until 360 years later, in 1969, that a massive, specially-built, icebreaking, diesel-powered supertanker, the *Manhattan,* crunched its way completely through the Northwest Passage.

Hudson wintered in a sheltered cove of the bay. As soon as the ice broke in the spring of 1611, he would have started exploring again, but his weary crew mutinied. Hudson, his young son, and seven men too ill to work were forced into a rowboat and left adrift there in the back of beyond. The mutineers decided to return to Europe, but they came to no happy end. Several were killed in a fight with Eskimos on their way down the bay, numerous others died of starvation, and the few who lived to reach England were thrown into prison. Nothing was ever heard of the marooned Hudson and his companions.

CAPTAIN JAMES COOK

The greatest of England's many great sea explorers was, without doubt, Captain James Cook, who once said of himself that he wanted "not only to go farther than anyone had done before, but as far as it was possible for man to go!" He just about did that, too, considering the ships and equipment of his time.

Cook's first major voyage started from England in late 1768. Besides his crew, Cook carried a number of passengers—all scientists, bound for the best spot in mid-Pacific from which to make certain astronomical observations and chart the transit of Venus. But Cook had another, quite secret, mission as well: to find and claim for England the great continent believed to lie in the far South Pacific. (Marco Polo had mentioned "hearing" of such a place.) So the scientists not only got to do their stargazing from Tahiti—at that time probably the single most beautiful island in the world—but they also got a real tour of much of the South Pacific. (While in Tahiti, incidentally, Cook's crewmen admired the artistic tattoos worn by the Tahitians which were pricked into their skin with sooty needles, and had similar adornaments applied to themselves—starting a custom still common among seamen.)

From Tahiti, Cook sailed to New Zealand (previously discovered by the Dutch), cruised around it and mapped it properly for the first time. Then he went on to New Holland (also discovered by the Dutch), sailed along a considerable length of its coast and claimed that for England. He then circumnavigated the Spanish-discovered New Guinea, proving it to be an island and not, as had been thought, an extension of New Holland. He continued westward, around Africa and back to England (in 1771). He believed, and so did the British Admiralty, that he had not found or taken possession of a great southern continent. He did not know that New Holland was not just one more of the countless Pacific islands, but that it was a continent, two-thirds as large as Europe. No one knew the vast extent of it. Indeed, the first man to cross the entire breadth of it was John MacDouall Stuart, in 1862, by which time it was known as Australia.

A year later Cook went looking for a great southern continent again—and once again he took along scientists, artists, and even a Scottish bagpiper for entertainment. (From all of his expeditions,

Cook and his passengers brought back thousands of new species of plants, fish, birds and insects, native tools and weapons, maps and drawings of each place visited—and once even a shrunken human head.) On this trip Cook quartered practically every square mile of the South Pacific, locating and mapping numerous islands previously glimpsed by others but known only by arbitrarily bestowed names, and discovering several new ones on his own: New Caledonia, Norfolk, the Isle of Pines. His was also the first ship to penetrate the Antarctic Circle, and he forged well south of it, in fact to within 1600 miles of the South Pole.

When Cook returned to England in 1775, he was given a soft, safe, salaried desk job, but this was not for Captain Cook. As biographer Alan Moorehead has written, "He was far gone with the

discoverer's disease, he had the habit of risk and he could not give it up." In less than a year Cook was off to sea again, on that same old explorers' quest for a Northwest Passage, but this time he would seek the western, or Pacific, end of the Passage. He provisioned at his favorite island of Tahiti, then sailed northeast and promptly discovered the Hawaiian Islands. (Actually, this may have been a rediscovery, for it seems the islands had been first noted by the Spanish explorer Juan Gaetano more than two hundred years before. Spain had not announced the discovery—choosing rather to wait until they could be colonized. But, in the meantime, Spain had somehow simply forgot about them.)

Cook went east to North America, sighting land at approximately where San Francisco is now, then he continued up the coast past Canada, around Alaska, through the Bering Straits and above the Arctic Circle. Thus Cook was the first explorer ever to see both the Antarctic and the Arctic, but there he, too, failed to find any sign of a sea passage to the Atlantic. He sailed south again, down the coast of Siberia including the Kamchatka Peninsula, and then returned to Hawaii. This was to be his last stop. A quarrel with the natives over a stolen longboat turned into a riot. Cook and his crewmen prudently withdrew toward the shore but, as soon as his back was turned, Cook was struck from behind. He fell, got up, struggled with the raging Hawaiians, was overpowered and beaten to death. On February 14, 1779, at the age of fifty, Captain James Cook at last had gone "as far as it was possible for man to go."

ALEXANDER MACKENZIE

Still the dream of a Northwest Passage across the North American continent continued to beguile explorers, even landlubbers. In 1779, a boy of about nineteen, named Alexander MacKenzie, came from Scotland by way of New York to seek his fortune in Canada. Within a couple of years, he was a partner in a fur-trading firm in Montreal, which later merged with other firms to form the great North West Company. Then he was appointed to head the North West Company's important Athabaska fur district, which was the farthest north and farthest west of the company's districts. This district was around Lake Athabaska in the remote wilderness where today the provinces of Alberta and Saskatchewan touch the Northwest Territory. MacKenzie's little Fort Chipewyan was 1800 miles in a straight line from the company headquarters at Montreal—probably twice that by dogsled, horse and canoe. This great distance made it very difficult to keep the trading post supplied and to ship out its collected furs. MacKenzie decided that on the whole it would be much easier to send furs and receive supplies via a Pacific port. So, like so many others before him, in 1789, MacKenzie set out with a team of men to seek a Northwest Passage.

He went, understandably, northwest by canoe along the Slave River to Great Slave Lake, discovered just eighteen years earlier and not yet mapped. There MacKenzie discovered that the immense lake emptied into a previously unknown river: a wide and navigable river flowing briskly northwest. Today this river bears MacKenzie's name. The explorer eagerly followed it for more than a thousand miles, and found that it did debouch into an ocean—the gray, icy, forbidding Arctic Ocean—but with the whole bulk of Alaska between him and the Pacific Ocean. Disappointed, MacKenzie returned to Fort Chipewyan, only to start planning, preparing and resupplying for another try at reaching the Pacific.

The next time, in 1793, he and his party canoed to the southwest, up the Peace River, into the Rocky Mountains from which the Peace River flows eastward. At its headwaters high in the Rockies they hoped to find—hopefully only a short portage away—the headwaters of some other stream flowing west toward the Pacific Ocean. And so they did: they found another hitherto undiscovered river, and canoed a short distance down it. But it proved to be too turbulent for their fragile craft—the river was full of rapids and cataracts—so they abandoned their canoe and started trudging overland. (That river would not be explored along its full length until Simon Fraser did it fifteen years later; it has been the Fraser River ever since.)

MacKenzie and his men crossed the whole Coast Range of mountains on foot, and descended the far slope to find themselves at last on the shore of the Pacific Ocean. They had not discovered any usable passage, but they were the first white men ever to cross the whole breadth of the North American continent north of Mexico. His account of his travels which was published in 1801 won him wide recognition and MacKenzie was knighted as Sir Alexander. In 1805 MacKenzie was elected to office in the Canadian Government, and was a leading figure in the development of the fur trade and other Canadian resources until, in 1808—having made his fortune, and famous as well—he returned to Scotland to live out his last years.

Lewis & Clark & Sacajawea

After MacKenzie the next white men to cross North America were U.S. Army Captain Meriwether Lewis and Lieutenant William Clark. Their three-year trek lasting from 1804 to 1806 took them from St. Louis, Missouri, to the Pacific coast of what is now Oregon, and back again. The Lewis and Clark expedition is better remembered than that of MacKenzie because it was more "romantic." Their party included a supposedly beautiful and undeniably dauntless Indian girl. She was a Shoshone named Sacajawea, one of the several wives of a French guide on the expedition. But it was she who did most of the guiding. In fact, Lewis and Clark would more than once have had to turn back if it hadn't been for Sacajawea's persuading other Indians to grant passage through their tribal territories, and to supply the explorers with food, horses and shelter. As mentioned earlier, the helpful Indians included the Nez Percé and other tribes who didn't realize that their hospitality to these travelers would eventually doom themselves to suppression, ouster from their ancestral lands, or outright extinction. Sacajawea is not, by her own race, exactly regarded as a heroine.

Henry Stanley & David Livingstone

Another explorer is best remembered for the remark he made at the conclusion of his hazardous and heroic safari through the African jungle. His many other exploits are all but forgotten, along with his real name. He was born John Rowlands, in Wales in 1841, but was orphaned while still very young, and at eighteen sailed as a cabin boy on a ship to New Orleans. There he was adopted and given a job by a kindly old American cotton broker named Henry Stanley, whose name John adopted at the old man's death.

From the moment of taking the new name, Henry Stanley was reborn—as an adventurer. The Civil War was just starting. He enlisted in the Confederate Army, was captured by the Yankees, and finagled his release from prison by enlisting on the Union side. He served in both the Union Army and Navy before the war was over. Then he traveled through the Wild West of America, and earned modest fame as a travel writer. His further journeys took him as far as Turkey and Tibet, before he returned to America to become a war correspondent reporting the U.S. Army's campaign against the Cheyennes. Stanley returned from the West to become a star reporter for the New York *Herald*. The newspaper sent him on assignments to Africa, Crete, Spain and France. Then, in 1871, in a grand gesture —the *Herald* had become New York's best-selling newspaper through just such gestures—the editor sent Stanley to lead a party into deepest Africa in search of an English explorer who had trekked into Africa five years before, had never been heard from since, and was presumed dead.

That man was the Reverend Doctor David Livingstone, who had

first come to Africa thirty years earlier to convert the natives to both Christianity and hygiene. Actually, he did more good as an explorer. During two separate stays in Africa, once for sixteen years, once for six, he had wandered over "the dark continent," charting its geography and river systems, and giving the world its first understanding of what, until then, had been a great blank on the map. Livingstone was over fifty, weary and wanting to retire, when he was persuaded to make his third journey into "darkest Africa." With a small party and not much in the way of supplies, he marched into the interior in April of 1866—and promptly disappeared.

In March of 1871, Stanley likewise plunged into the African interior. He spent eight months hacking his way through "forest, bush and jungle . . . nothing but miles and miles, endless miles of forest," having encounters with wild animals, wilder natives, snakes, insects, fever, and all the other hazards with which the jungle is infested, all the time following no firmer directions than native rumors and hints. Then he came at last to the village of Ujiji on the shore of Lake Tanganyika, and there found the lost missionary, emaciated by fever and malnutrition, but still alive. Stanley strode up to him and as casually as if they were meeting on a London street, he made the remark still famous and still quoted: "Doctor Livingstone, I presume?"

Stanley nursed Livingstone back to health, and the two explored together around Tanganyika for a while before Stanley, unable to persuade the doctor to return with him, returned to civilization to report Livingstone alive. Livingstone stayed on, making new discoveries and maps until, one morning in 1873, his native bearers found him kneeling in an attitude of prayer beside his tent cot—he was dead. Stanley had brought out with him Livingstone's invaluable earlier journals and maps, and thereafter, he too was obsessed with the notion of opening up Africa.

From 1874 to 1877, Stanley led a joint Anglo-American expedition to explore the length of the Congo River. Stanley's report that the river was navigable all the way to the heart of the continent, and his surmise that that part of Africa was teeming with untapped resources greatly interested the greedy King Leopold II of Belgium. The king hired Stanley to go back to the Congo region in 1879 and —though Stanley welcomed this simply as an opportunity to do more wandering through his beloved Africa—his explorations in truth gave Leopold the excuse to claim all the territory Stanley covered.

The king announced the formation of the Congo Free State under Belgian "protection"—and proceeded to turn it into his personal and private slave state. The Congolese blacks were put to forced labor, beaten, starved, tortured—all to make them bring out more of the Congo's wealth of ivory, rubber, palm oil and cacao for Leopold's enrichment. It was not until 1908 that other nations, outraged by these atrocities, formed an international commission which forced Leopold to cease his barbarities. And it was not until 1960 that Belgium finally loosed its stranglehold and granted the Congo independence. The nation has since adopted the native name of Zaïre.

But back to Stanley. He made still another exploration—this time in East Africa under British sponsorship—which won him reinstatement as a British subject, a knighthood, and election to Parliament. Though he revisited the United States and Africa on lecturing tours and visited Australia and New Zealand, he spent his remaining years mostly on his modest estate in Surrey, England. The stone over his grave there is engraved simply with his name and dates, "Henry Morton Stanley, 1841–1904," along with the name his native bearers gave him, *"Bula Matari,"* and below that, the one word "Africa."

CAPTAIN ROBERT SCOTT

"If I should die . . ." wrote the English poet Rupert Brooke, who did die, much too young, in the First World War:

> If I should die, think only this of me:
> That there's some corner of a foreign field
> That is for ever England . . .

That could be the epitaph of another English hero, who lies buried in a most foreign and unfriendly field 11,000 miles from his birthplace in England. This is Robert Falcon Scott of the Royal Navy, who, in 1900, sailed to the Antarctic, where he sounded the depth of the Ross Sea, discovered (under all the ice and snow) the land areas of Edward VII Peninsula and Victoria Land, and explored on foot to a new "farthest south" inland, just six hundred miles from the Pole. Ten years later, he sailed again, this time determined to be the first man to reach the South Pole, and to plant the British flag there. (The North Pole had been reached just a year earlier by the American explorer Robert Peary)

Scott set up his main base on the bleak shore of the Ross Ice

Shelf, then, with four companions, headed due south while dragging sledges of supplies. They had to climb mountains, bridge or circle around great crevasses, fight through wind and blowing snow—all in subzero temperatures. After two months, on January 18, 1912, they staggered to that invisible point which is the earth's South Pole—only to find, heartbreakingly, that it was no longer invisible. The flag of Norway had been planted there, just 35 days before, by explorer Roald Amundsen, who made a faster trek by dogsled and on skis from the Bay of Whales.

"Great God! This is an awful place," Scott noted in his journal; then the five discouraged Englishmen turned back toward their base. Their traveling was slowed by illness, frostbite and debilitating hunger (recurring blinding snowstorms made them miss the caches of canned food and fuel they had left along the way). On February 17, Petty Officer Edgar Evans died of sheer fatigue. On March 17, when the remaining four were huddled in a tent, sheltering from a blasting blizzard, their food all but finished, Captain Lawrence Oates said calmly, "I'm just going outside for a bit, chaps. I shan't be long." He was the feeblest of the four, and the others knew he was sacrificing himself so they could have more rations apiece and move faster. He never came back. The other three—Captain Scott, Lieutenant H. R. Bowers and Dr. E. A. Wilson—managed ten miles before another blizzard howled down on them.

Numerous rescue parties had set out from the Ross Shelf main base, and were repeatedly turned back by blizzards. It was not until November that the searchers found the ice-encrusted tent with its three frozen heroes—and Captain Scott's journal, ending in these painfully scrawled lines: "Had we lived, I should have had a tale to tell of the hardihood, endurance and courage of my companions which would have stirred the heart of every Englishman. These rough notes and our dead bodies must tell the tale."

Balto

While we're on the subject of adventures in the far regions of snow and ice, let me mention one hero who wasn't even human. He was a dog—an Eskimo malemute sled dog called Balto, the lead dog in a team belonging to an Alaskan fur trapper named Kasson.

In 1925, the town of Nome, in northwestern Alaska, was stricken with an epidemic of diphtheria. Four people died and twenty-five more were dying when the local doctor sent a desperate radio appeal for antitoxin to combat the disease. The SOS was heard in the town of Anchorage, and a doctor there hastily packed a 20-pound supply of the antitoxin serum. This was quickly hustled aboard a special express train. In those days, however, the only railroad line ran north and south between Anchorage and Fairbanks, with the train's closest approach to Nome being 650 trail miles distant.

A second radio call alerted all the men in the area who owned dogsleds to station themselves at intervals between the railroad and Nome. On the evening of January 27, the first sled driver (or "musher") met the train at the whistle-stop of Nenana, took the package and hurried westward. He and his dogs staggering from fatigue, he turned the package over to a second musher at noon the next day. And so it went, one musher after another nearly killing himself and his dogs to reach the next station. The last musher on station was Kasson. When he received the package, the temperature was 30 degrees below zero and snow was beginning to fall. Though anxious to move, Kasson waited a while in hope that the snow would let up. It didn't; it got heavier. Kasson buckled on his snowshoes, took the sled grips, cracked his whip, and Balto, followed by twelve other dogs harnessed two by two, strained into the traces.

Alternately trotting on his clumsy snowshoes and riding the sled's runners, Kasson kept the dogs lunging into the snow and biting wind. They plowed through snowdrifts, climbed icy hills, sometimes broke through skim ice on a running stream and had to slosh through the bitter cold water. Night came down, and Kasson could no longer see the landmarks of the trail. He could only follow the sled, and trust Balto to follow the scent of the trail. Once, the sled overturned, the antitoxin package fell off, and Kasson had to grope in the dark to find it and tie it more securely. Just as dawn was beginning to pale the sky, Nome came into view far ahead, and the dogs—"dog-tired" is the only expression—seemed imbued with new strength. Almost proudly, they cantered down the main street, and from every building came pouring the people of Nome, hurrahing and applauding. The team stopped at the doctor's house, and the dogs and driver alike slumped exhausted into the snow of the street.

The package of serum had traveled the 650 miles from trackside at Nenana to Nome in five and a half days. That trail had never before been traversed in less than nine days. Of course, all mushers were equally to be praised for rescuing Nome from the epidemic, but their names are all forgotten (nowhere can I learn Kasson's first name), while the dog Balto is still remembered as one of Alaska's great heroes. And even in New York City, 4,600 miles away, in Central Park, you can still see a bronze statue of Balto "who carried the serum to Nome."

CHARLES LINDBERGH

The most popular, beloved, lionized and raved-about American hero of all was Charles A. Lindbergh, the handsome, modest, Midwestern air-mail pilot who, at the age of twenty-five, flew alone across the Atlantic Ocean from New York to Paris in May of 1927. It later became legend, still believed by many people, that Lindbergh—"Lucky Lindy," or the "Lone Eagle," as he came to be called—was "the first to fly the Atlantic." Actually, more than twenty people had done it before him, in multi-engined airplanes or in dirigibles. Lindbergh was the first to do it *alone,* and in a tiny, new and untested single-engine monoplane, "The Spirit of St. Louis."

The plane was really a flying gas tank; Lindbergh took along no personal equipment—not even a parachute—just four sandwiches and two canteens of water. Heavily laden with 451 gallons of gasoline, the Ryan monoplane almost did not even get off the ground on take-off; it barely cleared a tractor and some telephone wires at the end of the runway on Long Island's Roosevelt Field. When Lindbergh landed at Paris, thirty-three hours later, he was mobbed by adoring Frenchmen at Le Bourget airfield; every newspaper in the world broke out front-page banner headlines; on his return to New York he was given a hero's "ticker-tape parade" up Broadway. He was presented with the Medal of Honor, the first Distinguished Flying Cross ever awarded, France's Cross of the Legion of Honor, and the British Royal Air Force Cross. Years later he won, as well, the Pulitzer Prize for his 1953 book recounting the epic flight.

Lindbergh never did really like publicity; one time he said he was "filled up with listening to this hero stuff." He married and moved to a remote New Jersey estate to escape the limelight. But here it glared even more mercilessly when his baby son was kidnapped and killed in 1932. Lindbergh thereafter loathed publicity even more. Many people like their heroes to be eminently visible,

and Lindbergh's stubborn refusal to preen and posture in public turned them against him. When he spoke out against the United States' getting involved in the Second World War, they viciously accused him of being pro-Nazi and a "Hitler lover." They did not know—not many people do even now—that, when America did get into the war, Lindbergh wangled an assignment to the Pacific as a "civilian advisor" and there flew 50 combat missions and downed at least two Japanese warplanes.

All his life, Lindbergh continued to contribute to the development of aviation; he helped design the Boeing 747 jumbo jet and worked on secret space projects for the U.S. Government. Late in life, he became an "eco-activist" dedicated to preserving the earth's environment. He fought for a ban on whale-hunting and, despite his love for flying, campaigned against the building of a supersonic transport plane (SST) because it would be an air polluter, a fuel-gulper and intolerably noisy.

In August of 1974, Charles Lindbergh, aged seventy-two, died of cancer. When he knew he had only a few days left to live, he had himself flown from a New York hospital to his favorite spot on earth, an isolated beach cottage on the Hawaiian island of Maui. There, attended only by his family, a few close friends and his Hawaiian neighbors, he was buried (wearing work clothes) in a plain wooden coffin made by local workmen—leaving the world as quietly as he had always wanted to live in it.

The Great Minds

Towering genius disdains a beaten path.
It seeks regions hitherto unexplored.
—Abraham Lincoln

There are numerous proverbial sayings, such as "brain over brawn," "the pen is mightier than the sword" and the like, which attest to the fact that heroism is not always dependent on bulging biceps, cavalier courage or the wielding of weapons. Many men and women have gone down in history—or even changed history—by sheer force of an extraordinary mind or will.

AKHENATON

The first of these of whom we have historical evidence was the Egyptian pharaoh Amenhotep IV. Like Moses, who completed the conversion of the Israelites from idolizing a whole catalogue of gods to the worship of one supreme Lord God Jehovah, Amenhotep also conceived the idea of a single, all-powerful god, but he did it a hundred years before Moses.

When Amenhotep came to the throne, about 1378 B.C., his people worshipped numerous gods, great and small. Chief among them

145

was Amon, "the hidden one," and most pharaohs took their names from that god; Amenhotep, for instance, meant "he in whom Amon is content." But the pharaoh, after long meditation, came to the conclusion that all the known world and all the visible universe had really been created by and was watched over by a Power far greater than any of the popular Egyptian gods; in fact, greater than all of them put together. That god, Amenhotep decided, was all-knowing, all-seeing and was manifest in all things. The god was simply too vast and unimaginable to be represented by any carved image or idol, so Amenhotep chose the sun—Aton, "the radiant disk"—to be the god's visible symbol.

Amenhotep announced to his people that his new god, Aton, would henceforth be their only god—and that he himself was changing his name to Akhenaton, "the effective spirit of Aton." He moved the capital of Egypt from Thebes (which had always been dedicated to Amon) two hundred and fifty miles farther down the Nile River, where he built an entire new city, Akhetaton, "the horizon of Aton." He commanded that throughout Egypt the name "Amon" —and even every plural reference to "the gods"—should be chipped off every temple, obelisk, crypt and pillar. For a while the mass of Egyptians were dismayed, confused and resentful. But they were not half so resentful as the numberless priests of the old gods, who suddenly found themselves unemployed, stripped of the privileges, luxury, respect and obedience they had formerly enjoyed. The priests railed against this "heretic" pharaoh, and predicted dire disaster for everyone who abandoned the old religion. But gradually the mass of people realized how much better off they were—materially, anyway—in that they no longer had to provide expensive sacrifices for all those other gods and pay extortionate tribute to the old gods' priests.

Akhenaton's religious upheaval also affected other aspects of Egypt's culture. He had his architects build Aton's temple at Akhetaton spacious and open so as to let the sun flood in—compared with the dark, secretive temple of Amon at Thebes, designed to overawe the worshippers with Amon's ominous power. Akhenaton encouraged Egypt's artists to carve their statues and paint their murals according to what they saw, rather than to follow the stiff, unnatural rules of the past. Previous pharaohs and other notables had always been portrayed as handsome and heroic. Akhenaton insisted that his court artists show him as he was—not twenty feet tall and noble-looking, as earlier pharaohs had been represented. He had a bulging head with a lantern jaw, a scrawny neck, narrow shoulders, a pot belly, and fat buttocks dwindling down to toothpick legs. That's the way he looked and that's the way he was portrayed by the court artists and craftsmen. This could hardly be called an artistic boon to posterity, but the new "natural" style of art did preserve for us one of the most beautiful women who ever lived. She was Akhenaton's queen, aptly named Nefertiti, meaning "Lo, the lovely one comes."

This new Egypt of an all-loving god, of freedom and beauty, was doomed, however, to blossom for only a brief twelve years. Had this monotheism endured, the whole course of history might have been different—and better. When Akhenaton was crowned, he inherited what was then the largest empire in the world, and the first that enjoyed stability through a firm central government. The Egyptian rule extended from Syria in the north, through Palestine and Egypt, to Nubia in the south. But Akhenaton became so involved with his reforms that he ignored state matters, and the empire suffered. The Hittites grabbed Syria. Wandering nomad tribes took over Palestine. All this gave the deposed priests the excuse they needed to stir up the Egyptian people against Akhenaton. Obviously, said the priests, the old gods were taking revenge by destroying the unbelievers. And the people agreed. Egypt was torn by riots and unrest. Finally even Akhenaton realized he would have to make a strategic retreat in order to preserve what was left of his empire. He elevated his teenaged son-in-law to be co-ruler with him, and gradually but unhappily faded into the background. The son-in-law boldly took the name Tutankhamen, "living image of Amon," and moved the capital back to Thebes. He urged the people to resume their worship of Amon and the other old gods. Akhenaton saw his warm and loving Aton denied, his reforms reversed, his dreams demolished—and he died, evidently of a broken heart, when he was only about thirty years old.

MARTIN LUTHER

Twenty-nine centuries after Akhenaton, another religious revolution—begotten in the mind of another dedicated man—did succeed in changing a long-entrenched religion, not in just one country, but in the whole western world.

In the Middle Ages, the Christian Church had become something quite different from what Jesus Christ had visualized. The faith that he taught had been very simple—mainly that men should love God and one another—a faith uncomplicated by "musts" and "don'ts" and "gimmes." In the course of fifteen centuries, however, the Church had elaborated those simple teachings into a complex system of principles, rules and demands, ranging from hairsplitting interpretations of what Christ had really meant, to the proper procedure for torturing and burning anyone who disagreed with the Church's system. The pope was the leader of the Church, and the infallibility of the Church was invested in him when he spoke *ex cathedra* on matters of faith and morals. The Church itself had become politically powerful, wealthy, able to raise its own armies, able to make or break kings and empires. None of the Church's actions could be questioned, no matter how un-Christian or even corrupt those actions might be. The Church was not to be criticized, but it was—by one perceptive and courageous priest named Martin Luther.

In the early 1500's, Father Martin Luther was a professor at the Church college in Wittenburg, Germany. As a hobby, he began to study the original Greek and Hebrew texts of the Bible. The more he studied the more he puzzled over the differences between the recorded words of Christ and those preached by the pope and his bishops. In 1511, Luther visited Rome, and there got a second shock. The pope was alternating his time between fighting a war with Venice and building a new and grandiose St. Peter's Church. Luther thought the church a flamboyant mockery of the simple places—fields, marketplaces, lake shores—which Christ had found adequate for his teaching. Luther also thought a pope should be a pious and holy man, not a scheming war commander.

What actually sparked Luther's criticism of the Church, however, was its practice of selling "indulgences." This requires a little explanation. All Christians then believed—as Roman Catholics still do today—that when a person dies, his soul is sent to purgatory for a period of "purification" before it can enter heaven. Purgatory is alleged to be an unpleasant and uncomfortable place, and believers hope their souls won't have to spend much time there. By acquiring a papal indulgence while he's still alive (through doing good works or making a significant contribution to the Church) a person could receive a "guarantee" (called an "indulgence") that when he died his soul would languish only briefly in that gray purgatory, and then could hurry on to eternal bliss in heaven. Well, the building of St. Peter's Church turned out to be fantastically more expensive than anyone had expected, and Pope Leo X found he was running out of money. So he hit on the notion of raising funds by selling indulgences written on pieces of parchment to anyone who wanted and could afford one. Indeed, he sent "salesman" priests into every part of Europe to convince people who had never heard of indulgences that for the sake of their souls they couldn't afford to be without one.

Martin Luther thought these tactics were atrocious, and said so. He wrote out a list of "ninety-five theses," criticizing the sale of indulgences and other abuses of Church power, and in October, 1517, he tacked this list to the Wittenberg "bulletin board," the door of the local church. Somewhat to Luther's surprise, other priests and even laymen copied his list of criticisms and circulated their copies to others. In less than two months, all Europe was discussing, analyzing, taking sides for or against Luther's ninety-five theses. Naturally, the pope heard of this growing commotion, and ordered Luther to come to Rome and explain his action. Luther, well aware of what had happened to Jan Hus a century earlier, refused—and was instantly excommunicated. When he received the notice, he made a ceremony of burning it in the Wittenberg square, to the loud admiration of the crowd.

From that moment on, willy-nilly, Luther was the leader of the many discontented, previously meek and silent, Christians in Europe. Giving voice to their protests against the Church, they became known as Protestants. The books Luther wrote to explain his ideas in more detail became best-sellers. His Wittenberg students, and those in other colleges, offered to become his personal army. The Church could not ignore this Protestant ground-swell; it called an assembly of Church elders, and Luther was again commanded to attend. By this time, he was so well known and widely admired that the Church would not have dared any treachery, as it had with Hus, so Luther went. Only to insist that he would not recant or renege on anything he had done, said or written. The convention thereupon declared Luther an outlaw before man and God, forbade all Christians to give him shelter or sustenance, or to read any of his books. This edict was so outrageous, however, that it served to turn many of the formerly loyal Church adherents into Protestants.

The Church of those times still exists, happily much modified, and now called the Roman Catholic Church to distinguish it from other Christian churches. There never did exist a single, unified Protestant Church, because Luther's revolt inspired imitation by other dissenters—such men as John Calvin in France, Ulrich Zwingli in Switzerland, and others—and each gathered his own adherents. Thus, almost as soon as Protestantism came into being, it was fragmented into numerous denominations of slightly or even widely differing beliefs—Lutherans, Calvinists, Anglicans, and so on—and even these main bodies later developed splinter sects. At last count, there were eighty-three major Protestant denominations—from Adventists to Wesleyans—practicing in the United States alone, with most of these being subdivided into numerous minor offshoots.

The Reformation, as Luther's era is called, caused a lot of enmity between Catholics and Protestants, and even a good deal of brother-against-brother religious warfare, killings, church burnings, and other atrocities. But it also gave Christians the backbone to resist the abuses of "God-given" authority, and to decide in what manner they wanted to worship God and Christ. For the first time in Christian history, they had the option of choice. Martin Luther, never as strong in body as in mind, was in poor health during the last ten years of his life. Nevertheless, he continued to travel and preach, until his last trip, in 1546, which took him through such foul weather that he caught a killing illness. A friend asked him, on his death-bed, whether he would die steadfast in the Protestant doctrines he had taught. Luther answered ringingly—it was his last word—"Yes!"

LEONARDO DA VINCI

Another man, who lived about the same time, never questioned the doctrines of the prevailing Church—religion was one of the few things in which he took little interest—but he questioned almost every other aspect of the universe. Of everything that caught his attention he asked "How does it work?" and "Why?" and he found out. He mastered more different branches of art and science than has any man before or since. There has never been another genius like him: brilliant as a diamond, and as multi-faceted.

Leonardo da Vinci was born in the city-state of Florence (in what is now Italy), the son of a small-time lawyer and a peasant girl; whence his genius came is a mystery. From early childhood on he showed a remarkable talent in painting, music and sculpture. At the age of fourteen he was apprenticed to a master painter, and by the age of twenty he was a master himself and registered in the painter's guild. He became renowned as one of Europe's greatest painters and, even in his own lifetime, was eventually recognized as the foremost of all. Of his works that have survived, probably the greatest is the fresco "The Last Supper," which took him three years

to paint on a monastery refectory wall. Certainly his most famous painting—copied and reproduced more times than any other picture ever made—is that of Lisa, the wife of Zanobi del Giocondo. The painting is known as *La Gioconda* or *The Mona* [meaning "Madonna"] *Lisa*. It is said that Leonardo worked on it at intervals over four years and that every time the lady Lisa sat to pose, he kept musicians playing to inspire that indescribable expression ("the Gioconda smile") on her face.

Leonardo was also kept busy doing sculpture for various patrons and lending his help as architect on several churches. But it was not until centuries after his death, when his notebooks and journals were deciphered, that the true and limitless extent of his genius became known. None of his family and friends who inherited these documents paid them much attention, nor did the institutions in which they later reposed—because nobody could read them. Leonardo was left-handed (which alone makes him something of a rarity among artists) and it amused him to set down his writings backward, in such a way that they could be read only by holding them up to a mirror.

From his notes and diaries, we have learned much more about the man. For example, most artists learn to paint people by practicing drawing nude models. Leonardo went further; he went into hospitals and dissected dead bodies, to learn exactly how human muscles and sinews and tendons work and how they affect a person's appearance. He was just as thorough in investigating other subjects that caught his interest—and he was interested in almost everything. He studied mathematics, architecture, engineering, geology, botany, hydraulics, geography, mechanics, mapmaking until he was expert. He put his knowledge to uses one would not expect of an artist. He planned and supervised the building of irrigation systems for farm fields and sewage systems for cities. He designed canals to keep the Arno River from devastating Florence with its floods; he built drains that dried the swamps of central Italy, thus ending the plagues regularly spread by the mosquitoes bred there.

He became interested in other subjects in which there were no experts, so that he was the first to study and master them. There were, for instance, no meteorologists in those days, until Leonardo became one by studying the phenomena of weather, storms and lightning. He studied ocean tides, the movements of rivers, the structure of mountains, the causes of landslides and ways to prevent them. He was centuries ahead of James Watt, inventor of the steam engine, in speculating on the uses of steam power. Leonardo was sure that steam under pressure could fire a more powerful cannon than could gunpowder, but he refused to design a steam cannon because he was against war. Likewise, he claimed to have found a way for a man to stay under water indefinitely, but he wouldn't reveal that, either, because of "the evil nature of man." His most farsighted ventures, however, were in the then-unheard-of field of aviation. Leonardo studied the flight of birds, and sketched designs for aircraft—even a helicopter—which he could probably have built and made to fly, if there had then existed any practical sort of engine.

As one biographer has written, Leonardo had "the passion of knowledge for its own sake." In art, he surpassed all previous artists. In science, he was a pioneer of scientists to come. Leonardo was not just a drudge, however, he led a full life. In youth, he was well-built, handsome, golden-haired, and much admired for his good humor, his feats of strength and horsemanship, his eloquent conversation. In his later years, he was revered and adored by those students and apprentices—including princes and nobles—who came to sit at his feet and imbibe his wisdom. At the end, in 1519, aged sixty-seven, he died as cheerfully as he had lived. He once said, "As a day well spent gives joyful sleep, so does a life well spent give joyful death."

Queen Elizabeth I

Even in the olden days, long before the "women's liberation movement," men had no monopoly on genius, any more than they did on bravery, loyalty, talent, patriotism or any other virtue. Then, as now, any outstanding woman would be recognized as such, without her having to demand that her abilities be noticed. For example, in 1558, though there were numerous well-qualified male claimants to the throne of England, Elizabeth I was crowned, simply because the English people had long admired her as a princess and now wanted her as their queen.

Other nations soon realized that this woman possessed the wisest and shrewdest mind of any monarch of the time. Elizabeth once said, "I know I have the body of a weak and feeble woman, but I have the heart and stomach of a king, and of a king of England at that." More self-confident words could hardly be spoken. Elizabeth never married, and was called the Virgin Queen (hence our state of Virginia, named in her honor), but she made many an alliance, favorable to England, by flirting with foreign princes and hinting that she might someday marry one of them.

When Elizabeth came to the throne, England was at low ebb. The country was ridden with debt. It was shamed by a recent defeat in a war with France. It had had a succession of alternately Protestant and Catholic rulers, whose effect had been to foment strife between Englishmen of different beliefs. Elizabeth immediately began soothing England's troubles—first by improving its financial situation. Without actually declaring war on any nation, she quietly promoted the numerous English pirates to "privateers," encouraged them to prey on Spanish and Dutch shipping, and saw to it that the national treasury was enriched by a healthy share of their booty.

Elizabeth made the (Protestant) Church of England the national religion, which it still is, yet she allowed everyone to worship differently who wanted to do so. She encouraged exploration, and her seafarers established the first outposts of the British Empire to be. Sir Humphrey Gilbert claimed Newfoundland for her. Sir Walter Raleigh landed the first English colonists in Virginia, and planted the British flag in Guiana in South America. Sir Francis Drake claimed "New Albion" on North America's west coast, though that claim was not followed by colonization (New Albion is today San

Francisco, California). Elizabeth also encouraged learning and the arts; her reign produced playwright William Shakespeare, poet Edmund Spenser, philosopher Francis Bacon, among other notables.

Then King Philip II of Spain declared war on England. Elizabeth had long since ceased to pretend that she had nothing to do with the pirates looting Spanish ships and colonies, and now Philip decided the time had come to squash the growing English menace. He sent the mighty Spanish Armada of warships to sweep the ocean clean of English vessels and to invade England itself. As we know, the "invincible" Armada was defeated—not by Elizabeth, of course, but partly by her captains Sir Francis Drake and Sir John Hawkins, and mainly by a timely hurricane. Elizabeth got the credit, however, when the English hurrahed, "Britannia rules the waves!"

Elizabeth could rightly have taken credit for a lot of other good things: laws she had passed to help the poor and protect the working people, a fat and growing treasury, an England of peace and prosperity, and a British Empire rapidly expanding over the world. Still, in her last days, discussing with her court ladies a possible epitaph for her gravestone, she said, "I only desire that my name shall be recorded in a line or two, which shall briefly express my name, my virginity, the years of my reign, the reformation of religion under it, and my preservation of peace." Instead, her name resounds through history books as the most accomplished woman, most successful ruler and most astute mind (male or female) of her time.

KAMEHAMEHA, KING OF HAWAII

After meeting such people as Elizabeth, Leonardo and Luther, it may be difficult to conceive of an illiterate, uneducated, unskilled and near-naked "savage" as being in the same category of "great minds." Such there have been, however. In 1782, a young man of twenty-four, named Kamehameha, became king of the island of Hawaii. Only three years before, his fellow Hawaiians had murdered Captain Cook and made it plain that foreigners were unwelcome. But Kamehameha realized that more voyagers would come. He knew next to nothing of the outside world, but he did know that it would encroach upon the islands, and that the islands were ill-prepared to cope.

At that time, the eight main, inhabited islands of the group were divided among four kingdoms. Kamehameha knew they must be united for their own good, so he united them by the only means he

knew: He conquered the three other kings, one after another. Thereafter, he laid aside his weapons and took up the scepter of government. He welcomed some visiting foreigners and banned others. He
resisted Russian attempts to annex the islands, got rid of Spanish
pirates by refusing to supply their ships, and allowed the settlement
of those who brought useful plants, animals, arts and industries.
(When one group of settlers built a distillery, King Kamehameha
tried their liquor. He got drunk, which he liked; suffered a hang-
over, which he didn't like; and banished both the distillery and the
distillers.)

While he lived, Kamehameha performed the incredible juggling
act of keeping his kingdom free and independent, taking what he
wanted of the modern world and rejecting the rest—a performance
unmatched by many a skilled, learned, worldly-wise and "civilized"
European ruler. After Kamehameha's death in 1819, the islands suffered from intruders who came with good intentions as well as those
who came with ulterior motives. Benign missionaries and fugitive
criminals, respectable tradesmen and unscrupulous fortune-hunters,
hard workers and worthless beachcombers—all tended to undermine the ancient Hawaiian religion, morals, freedom and joys of the
simple life, and to introduce instead oppression and exploitation,
vice and disease.

SEQUOYAH

At about that same time, but some five thousand miles away, and
in a rather different manner, another prodigiously intelligent "savage" was helping unite his people against the white man's depre-
dations. In the early 1800's, the Cherokees were the largest tribe of
Indians in North America, or, more accurately, a loose confedera-
tion of groups which lived in the Carolinas, Georgia, Alabama and
Tennessee. They had a spoken language, of course, but no written
language beyond picture symbols. They regarded the white people's books and newspapers with awe, and referred to them as "the
talking leaves."

One who realized the importance and advantages of the talking
leaves was a Cherokee named Sequoyah. (Actually he was the son
of a Cherokee woman and a white trader, and was known to the
whites as George Guess.) Sequoyah was a trader himself for a while,
but then, crippled in an accident, he became a silversmith. Leading a sedentary life of considerable leisure, he began to puzzle over

ways to set down the Cherokee speech in writing. For twelve years, he spent his spare time moving pebbles and sticks around in various combinations, or scratching marks on stones. All his tribal mates, even his wife, thought he was "spirit-struck" (slightly loony).

Sequoyah began by trying to devise a separate symbol for every word in the Cherokee language, the cumbersome system used (though he couldn't have known it) by the Chinese. However, he soon gave that up as too unwieldy and, by trying a simpler system, in 1821 he finally succeeded. It is popularly believed that Sequoyah invented a "Cherokee alphabet." He didn't. He invented a "syllabary," or a separate symbol for each different syllable in the Cherokee tongue. This would be insuperably difficulty for a complex language like English, but Cherokee has only eighty-five different sounds, so Sequoyah needed only eighty-five symbols. Some of them he copied from the white men's alphabet, others he made up himself.

Still, the other Cherokees couldn't grasp what Sequoyah had accomplished until he gave a demonstration. At a crowded tribal meeting, Sequoyah had one high chief whisper a message to him; Sequoyah wrote it down in his invented syllabary, handed it to his small daughter and she read it aloud word for word. Once the Cherokees realized what a powerful new tool they had, they were all eager to learn to use it, and Sequoyah's writing spread throughout the vast Cherokee territory. With this new ease of communication, the innumerable Cherokee groups were able to unite, named themselves the Cherokee Nation, and set up a government along the lines of that of the United States. They even published parts of the Bible in the Cherokee language, and started a weekly Cherokee newspaper.

The white men later did some dastardly things to the Cherokees —stole their lands, herded them into the western wilderness—and the Cherokee Nation was disbanded in 1906. But the fact that it lasted as long as it did is mainly due to Sequoyah's invention, which made the Cherokee the most civilized Indian tribe ever to exist north of Mexico. Even the whites recognized Sequoyah's genius and accomplishment; when botanists discovered the giant redwood trees of California and Oregon, the tallest trees on earth, they named them "sequoia" in his honor.

BENJAMIN FRANKLIN

A contemporary of both Kamehameha and Sequoyah—though, of

course, he never met either of them—was Benjamin Franklin, the most universal genius the world has known since Leonardo da Vinci. As with Leonardo, it's a mystery whence came Franklin's inquiring and wide-ranging mind. He was the son of a humble soap and candle maker in Boston, and he never had more than a smattering of schooling. At the age of ten, he was working full time in his father's shop. That was (literally) stinking work, and he soon moved to his half-brother's printing shop, where was published the *New England Courant.* Franklin not only learned printing, he also secretly, under assumed names, contributed articles to the paper. This was probably the best schooling he could have had.

In 1723, at seventeen, Ben Franklin moved to the big city—Philadelphia—and by the age of twenty-four was owner, publisher and editor of the *Pennsylvania Gazette.* His sharp, witty and common-sense articles soon made the *Gazette* the most popular periodical in the colonies. In 1732, Franklin started, and published for twenty-five years, *Poor Richard's Almanack,* notable for its pithy observations on industriousness, thrift and good sense, many of which have since become "American proverbs." As if all this weren't enough occupation for one man, Franklin studied foreign languages, philosophy and science. He wrote books of his own, promoted those of other authors, set up America's first circulating library, founded the American Philosophical Society, and helped establish an academy which now is the University of Pennsylvania.

In 1748, Franklin turned all his publishing enterprises over to his foreman, and decided to spend the rest of his life as a scientist. In those days, a scientist did not need diplomas, degrees and a string of academic initials after his name; anybody could be a scientist, and Franklin certainly qualified. His famous and foolhardy experiment of flying a kite in a thunderstorm established for the first time that lightning is an electrical discharge, and enabled him to invent the lightning rod. He also invented the harmonica, bifocal eye-glasses, and the easily-built, cheap and practical "Franklin stove." He also invented such curiosa as frogman flippers (identical to those worn by scuba divers today), a one-handed clock, and a rocking chair whose motion powered a built-in fan.

Then Franklin got into politics—first as deputy postmaster general of the colonies, in which office he made the mail deliveries more rapid, efficient and profitable than they are in our present day of air mail, Zip codes, computers and all the other trappings of "modern science." Next, Franklin was made a diplomatic courier between the increasingly rebellious colonies and the mother country of England. He considered making his home in England—where his literary and scientific reputation had made him hugely popular—but the looming American Revolution brought him dutifully home to help as he might. Franklin became one of the "founding fathers" of the United States. He helped draft the Declaration of Independence; he was a delegate to the Continental Congress; he was sent in a vain attempt to get Canada to join the Revolution. Next he was sent as an emissary to France, where he succeeded in procuring extra troops and supplies for the American cause. (Incidentally, it is amusing and admirable that Franklin, though in his seventies, bald and fat, enjoyed an astounding number of romances among the lovely and sophisticated ladies of the French court. His solemn diplomatic reports from there are enlivened by many a good-humored squib of advice on how to woo and win a damsel.)

When the Revolution was won, Franklin went to England to help work out the details of the peace treaty. He eventually returned to America to help his fellow founding fathers write their most majestic and long-lasting document, the American Constitution. Franklin died in 1790, full of years (eighty-six) and honors. His gravestone would have had to be as high as the Washington Monument to list all his accomplishments, attainments and achievements. Instead, he asked that it read simply (and wittily):

The body of
Benjamin Franklin, printer,
(Like the cover of an old book,
Its contents worn out,
And stript of its lettering and gilding)
Lies here, food for worms!
Yet the work itself shall not be lost,
For it will, as he believed, appear once more
In a new
And more beautiful edition,
Corrected and amended
By its Author!

ALBERT EINSTEIN

The greatest scientific mind of modern times belonged without doubt to that genius of physics, Albert Einstein. After his death in

1955, a handwritten note was found among his papers. It evidently had been scribbled sometime in his youth, for it said, "Something deeply hidden had to be behind things." Einstein searched all his life for that "something deeply hidden"—and found it, and demonstrated how that "something" accounts for the existence and behavior of all things in Creation.

Whatever subject a scientist studies, he attempts first to find out all the facts about it, then to deduce from those facts a system or mechanism or natural law that accounts for them. By the time Einstein was born (in 1879), physicists had accumulated masses of data about the subjects of light, optics, electricity, magnetism, gravity and a host of other fields of inquiry. But, in every one of these fields, phenomena kept cropping up that did not accord with the "established" facts. The scientists were somewhat in the position of an uninstructed man who knows that a telephone works, and that he can call a friend on it, but does not understand the dial system. Like that man, the scientists kept getting "wrong numbers."

Then along came Einstein. In person and personality, he was the

typical absent-minded professor, often forgetting even to tie his shoelaces (while perhaps wearing shoes of different colors). But that was because his mind was so busy elsewhere. It might be probing the submicroscopic regions of atomic particles too infinitesimal ever to be seen—or his mind might be ranging beyond the farthest stars, to the limits of the universe. Einstein never maintained the typical science laboratory: weird-looking machines, retorts, glass tubing and the like. He did all his work in his head, and with pencil on paper. (He might have done even more than he did, had he lived to work in our Age of Computers.) But he was humble about his genius. "The whole of science," he said, "is nothing more than a refinement of everyday thinking."

In 1905, he published his first "theory of relativity"—which, simply stated, deals with the relation of *everything* in the universe to *everything else*. It not only accounted for many of those "wrong numbers" other scientists kept getting in their work on one subject or another but it also laid the groundwork for an all-encompassing, unified theory which would show that all the concerns of physics— light, electricity, cosmic rays, magnetism, gravity, etc.—were interconnected and governed by the same set of natural laws. Einstein's several theories published over the years are far too complex to deal with here. At their first publication, it was said that there were only nine other men in the world who could really understand them. They were, and still are, far beyond the comprehension of nonphysicists.

To cite a couple of Einstein's innovations, he was bold enough to introduce into his calculations and theories a whole new factor, a "fourth dimension" that could not be seen, touched, felt—the dimension of *time*. Again, he proved that matter—you, me, the dirt, the stars—is a form of energy, and that energy is a form of matter, and that the relationship of the two forms can be reduced to a simple equation: $E = mc^2$, or "energy equals the mass multiplied by the speed of light multiplied by itself." I will not clutter this page with equations. Suffice it to say that, by Einstein's formula, it can be calculated that the atomic energy in a pound of helium would keep a ten-watt light bulb burning for one hundred million years. Or conversely, that it would take 315,360,000,000 kilowatts of electric power to manufacture a pound of helium. That is, if anyone knew how to manufacture it and could procure that much power—about five hundred times as much as is produced and used in all the United States in a solid year.

Einstein's theories were so spectacularly revolutionary that his name became known among laymen who couldn't even begin to comprehend his theories. For instance, every man in the street knew there were three dimensions—everything from an ant to a skyscraper has length, width and height—but to consider a fourth dimension was laughable. At the time Einstein became famous, there also lived a writer named Gertrude Stein and a sculptor named Jacob Epstein —which coincidence inspired some wit to pen this limerick:

> There's a marvelous family named Stein:
> There's Gert and there's Ep and there's Ein.
> Gert's writings are bunk,
> Ep's sculptures are junk,
> And nobody understands Ein!

To be serious again, Einstein completely reshaped and gave new impetus and direction to the science of physics. And lucky we are that he spent the last twenty years of his life in the United States. For his theories enabled others to develop the science of nuclear physics. In 1939, at the start of the Second World War, Einstein wrote to President Roosevelt and urged that he consider the possibility of constructing an atomic bomb. Roosevelt immediately set up the top-secret Manhattan Project, which did indeed produce the atomic bombs that wrote finis to that war. Although he had proposed the project, Einstein did not work on it for he loathed war. Still, our enemies might well have had the atomic bomb first if Einstein had been living in his native Germany at the time. But he was a Jew and had fled to America in 1934, when Hitler began persecuting, robbing, jailing and killing the Jews of Germany.

We owe much to Albert Einstein; his theories inspired future scientific development ranging from many of the life-enriching luxuries we enjoy today to our successful explorations in space. Most important, though, is the nuclear energy he helped put at our disposal. At this moment, it is lurking in rocket warheads, waiting to be unleashed in history's most destructive (and very possibly last) war. At the same time, it is fueling power plants which could turn the whole earth into a Garden of Eden. Only time will tell whether the war or peace aspect of nuclear energy will prevail. But it is ironic that the fate of all civilization, of the planet itself, rests on Einstein's insignificant-looking little equation: $E = mc^2$

Gentle Heroes

> Anyone who proposes to do good must not expect people to roll stones out of his way, but must accept his lot calmly if they even roll a few more upon it.
>
> —Albert Schweitzer

A *chapter* on the gentle heroes—those who influenced their part of the world or their time through love, greatness of soul, kindliness, generosity, nobility—could well include the founders and propounders of the world's leading religions: Abraham, Moses, Confucius, Christ, Mohammed and the Buddha. But those heroes belong in a different book. Here let us deal with the less than divine mortals with whom we human beings can more easily identify.

HAROUN-AL-RASCHID

If you have read the tales of Sinbad, Ali Baba and Aladdin in the *Arabian Nights,* you know that the wicked caliph is as much a standard villain as is the wicked stepmother in European fairy tales. But there was one caliph who was quite the opposite of wicked. His name was Haroun-al-Raschid (which translates as "Aaron the Upright"), and from his capital at Baghdad he ruled a tremendous Arabian empire during the years 786 to 809. His reign was the best, happiest and most prosperous the Arabs had enjoyed to that day—and maybe to this day.

Haroun-al-Raschid was a most devout Moslem. Scarcely a year went by that he did not make the arduous pilgrimage to worship at Mecca, the birthplace of Mohammed, and he inspired his people to follow the precepts of Mohammed: to be faithful to Allah, to be kind to beggars and strangers, never to gamble, cheat, slander or get drunk—in short, to be good and do right. Haroun was also a scholar and a poet. He supported struggling artists, writers, musicians, and encouraged wider education among his people. During his reign, Baghdad reached its highest peak of culture and remained, for five centuries thereafter, "the center of the civilized world." Haroun's fame as a wise and exemplary ruler spread even into Europe. Another goodhearted monarch, Charlemagne, corresponded with him, and the two became regular pen pals. At Charlemagne's request, Haroun granted permission—he was the only "infidel" ruler ever to do so without a fight—for Christians to come and visit Christian shrines in the Arab-occupied Holy Land.

Unlike most heads of government then and now, Haroun did not decide what was good for his subjects, nor did he rely on advisers who might tell him only what they thought he'd like to hear. Instead, Haroun went among his people—often alone, always in the disguise of a commoner—mingled with crowds in the marketplace, with worshippers in the mosque, with far travelers in the caravanserai (combined inn and camel stable). In such places he merely listened or asked an occasional discreet question, to learn the people's problems, complaints, grievances and their suggestions (if any) for solutions to their problems. Then, back in his palace outside Baghdad, he would set his jurists to composing new laws or improving the old ones. Toward the end of his reign, when Haroud visited a market, mosque or inn, he heard few complaints, but began hearing compliments instead, to the great and good Caliph Haroun "the Upright." He died young, at age forty-five, of a sudden malady, but he probably died happier than most rulers have done.

KING ALFRED THE GREAT

Just ninety years later, but 3,400 miles away, another man died who once had written, "My will was to live worthily as long as I lived, and, after my life, to leave, to them that should come after, my memory in good works." He was King Alfred of England, known to history as Alfred the Great. It is remarkable how much this northern, Saxon, Christian ruler resembled the eastern, Arab, Moslem Haroun-al-Raschid. Alfred was a warrior for much of his life. He had to be. When he came to the throne in 871, very little of England was English. The greater part of it was either continually being invaded or was already occupied by Danish Vikings. It took Alfred fully twenty-five years of seesaw warfare—victory, defeat, stalemate, victory—to drive the Danes from the land. But his most memorable deed was done after peace had been finally won. This was his success in restoring an England ravaged by the long Danish occupation.

During this period of almost unceasing warfare, the English had reverted nearly to the barbarism of Boadicea's day. There was no education beyond the arts of war, there were no laws beyond the brute law of self-survival, there was no Church to give spiritual guidance. Alfred, who himself had not learned to read English until he was twelve, was faced with the task of bringing order, justice and culture again to this wartorn land and brutalized people. This he did, however, and in just the four short years that he had left to him. (All his adult life Alfred had been afflicted with epilepsy, which sent him into sudden, violent fits, and about the year 900 he suffered his last and fatal attack.)

Alfred built monasteries, and sent a special mission to Rome to ask the pope to assign priests and monks to revitalize the Church in England. He established a "court school" at London for promising youths and clerics, in which mature noblemen were taught as well, and imported scholars from the Continent to teach in it. He learned Latin—a language known by few in England, but the language in which most books of the time were written—and himself translated into English, so that everyone might read, the best histories he could find, both of England and of the world, a manual of philosophy and several religious works. He also started what has since come to be called the *Anglo-Saxon Chronicle*, which was kept up by later scholars for more than two hundred years, and remains our most dependable history of that period.

After his death, Alfred became the hero of a multitude of invented legends, though none was needed to justify his being called "the Great." There could be no better summation of his life than the inscription on his statue, erected in his hometown of Wantage, Berkshire: "Alfred found learning dead, and he restored it; the laws powerless, and he gave them force; the Church debased, and he raised it; the land ravaged by a fearful enemy, from which he delivered it. Alfred's name shall live as long as mankind shall respect the past."

Probably the gentlest and most heroic of the world's gentle heroes was born about the year 1182 in a small town called Assisi, in what is now Italy. His name was Giovanni di Bernardone, but he was nicknamed Francesco ("Frenchman") because his father was a merchant who traveled frequently to France. Francesco is now most often referred to, in our language, as St. Francis of Assisi. For the first half of his life, Francis was anything but a saint. His father being well-to-do, Francis had no need to work; he enjoyed himself as a man-about-town. He dressed in dandified clothes, banqueted, drank, gambled, occasionally went soldiering just for a lark, caroused—and, in general, played the spoiled brat of a doting family. Then, at the age of twenty-four, he changed. As a biographer tells it, "One day he gave a banquet to his friends, and after it they sallied forth through the streets, Francis being crowned as king of the revelers; after a time they missed him, and on retracing their steps they found him in a trance, a permanently altered man."

He was an altered man indeed. He doffed his fashionable clothes, and with them went all his old bad habits. He put on rags, and with them came a new humility, a joyous religious fervor, a devotion to others' welfare, and a resolve to give to those needier than himself every copper he owned or could earn. For example, Francis had always a dread of those beggars afflicted with leprosy. There was one especially decayed and horrible beggar whom Francis had long shunned; now Francis went to him, gave him money, and even kissed the rotting stump of the leper's hand. Thereafter, though he did what he could to help all the ill and poor, Francis particularly devoted himself to helping lepers and raising funds for their hospitals.

Though he never took holy orders, nor was ordained a priest, Francis wandered over Italy, preaching his simple doctrine of humility, poverty, joy and helpfulness. Eventually there gathered around him a group of followers whom he had converted to his way of life, and Pope Innocent III gave the group permission to start a religious colony. The colony consisted only of huts built of scrap wood, clustered around a small chapel, but these impoverished preachers seldom inhabited the huts. They were forever on the move, carrying Francis' teaching to others. They worked as field hands to earn their daily bread, slept in barns or hedgerows, and whenever they earned a centesimo more than they needed, gave it to the poor.

Francis' own wanderings took him as far as Dalmatia, France, Spain, Egypt and the Holy Land. When he returned in 1221, he found that his little colony, now dignified by the name of the Franciscan Order, had become too numerous and unwieldy for him to administer and still continue his traveling and preaching. Had Francis remained leader of the order, he would have become a powerful figure in the Church, but he preferred his original humble mission, and handed over the order to other, more ambitious men.

Once again alone and on his own, Francis continued to grow in piety and popularity. He became known as a lover of all the "little things" in nature, and most of the statues erected to him have carved birds perched on his shoulders and small wild animals curled lovingly at his feet. It is a fact that once, on a hillside empty of any congregation but a flock of sparrows, Francis preached an impassioned sermon to the sparrows. He also referred to every natural phenomenon familiarly and respectfully: "brother Sun," "sister Moon," "brother Wind" and the like. In his final illness, a festering sore on his body had to be cauterized with a red-hot iron; Francis did not wince, but welcomed "brother Fire."

That illness lasted for two years of excruciating pain and almost total blindness, but Francis continued cheerfully, without complaint, to direct the good works of his disciples. His last words are usually quoted as "I have sinned against my brother the Ass," which doesn't make much sense. In actuality, he apologized to "brother Ass" (meaning his own body) for having abused it with starvation, exposure and self-denial for so many years, and wearing it out before its time. He was only forty-four years old. In recognition of this gentle hero's indisputable saintliness, the Church canonized him as Saint Francis a mere two years after his death. (The ceremony can sometimes—as in the case of St. Joan of Arc—be debated and delayed for centuries.) It was well and truly said of St. Francis of Assis that "probably no one has ever set himself so seriously to imitate the life of Christ and to carry out so literally Christ's work in Christ's own way."

Abraham Lincoln

To move down to more modern times, this sentence appeared in a *Chicago Times* editorial: "The cheek of every American must tingle with shame as he reads the silly, flat and dishwatery utterances of a man who has to be pointed out to intelligent foreigners as the President of the United States."

The disgraced Richard Nixon? No. The all but invisible and forgotten Millard Fillmore? No. That was an 1863 report of Abraham Lincoln's Gettysburg Address—which just shows how wrong some judgments can be. In the more than one hundred years since then, no public figure has been remembered, admired and venerated by his fellow Americans more than Abraham Lincoln. And it is impossible to foresee any public figure who is ever likely to displace him in the nation's esteem.

The English writer William Thackeray referred to Abraham Lincoln as "a gentle-man," and the hyphen was deliberate, because a mere "gentleman" could be anyone of good birth, good breeding or just good pocketbook. Lincoln was a man and he was gentle. Oh, he held his own in the fistfights and wrestling matches of his youth. He once enlisted in the Black Hawk Indian War (though he never saw action). And he was forceful enough in dealing with political opponents, incompetent underlings and indecisive generals. (He once sent a message to his bumbling General George McClellan: "I have just read your dispatch about fatigued horses. Will you pardon me for asking what the horses of your army have done that fatigues anything?") He could even be petty or perfidious at times; he was a human being, after all. But foremost among his qualities were charm, good humor and kindliness.

It is a wonder that Abe Lincoln grew up to be that gentle-man. His life was full of failures, disappointments and defeats, and he should by rights have been a bitter and vindictive man. He was left motherless at ten. His shiftless father could provide him with no more than a scant few years of schooling. He worked at such menial jobs as rail-splitter, flatboatman, surveyor's assistant. He tried running a general store, and went broke. By working at odd jobs, he managed to stay alive while he studied law under a lawyer friend. Finally he hung out his own shingle as a lawyer in Springfield, Illinois, got elected to the state legislature and even went to the U.S. Congress for one term. But he found the political offices frustrating and his performance in them was undistinguished.

Lincoln's personal life was as dismal as his professional life. For all his good-fellowship among men, he was homely, shy and too awkward to be a lady's man. When he proposed to one Mary Owens in 1838 and was turned down flat, he wrote to a friend, "I have now come to the conclusion never again to think of marrying, and for this reason: I can never be satisfied with anyone who would be block-head enough to have me." However, the next year, he attended a ball in Springfield, and was introduced to the pretty Mary Todd. He bowed to her and mumbled, "Miss Todd, I want to dance with you in the worst way." She recalled later that "he certainly did" (dance in the worst way). Despite Abe's shambling shyness, she eventually accepted his proposal and they were married in 1842.

It was a dreary marriage. Mary Todd was mentally unbalanced; in spells of depression she acted as if Abe did not exist; in spells of agitation she raged at him; many times she staged embarrassing scenes in public. Abe, though he once spoke of himself as "the most miserable man living," stood staunchly by Mary, while her condition worsened over the years. After Lincoln's death, when Mary's condition could no longer be discreetly concealed, a lunacy commission adjudged her insane. Also, of the Lincolns' four sons, three died before he did, and each of their deaths was another crushing blow to him. Yet Lincoln heroically surmounted all his despairs and despondencies to attend to his legal business, his political affairs and his ambitions. He finally attained the utmost height, the Presidency, but even this did not make him vain or arrogant or self-congratulatory. Regard his spur-of-the-moment speech to some visiting soldiers, on leave from the war: "I beg you to remember this. I happen temporarily to occupy this big White House. I am a living witness that any one of your children may look to come here, as *my* father's child has."

It is a wonder that Lincoln developed his sympathetic attitude toward the blacks, defended their interests, and finally freed them from two and a half centuries of slavery. I say "wonder" because Abe's earliest encounter with Negroes was hardly calculated to make him sympathetic. At the age of nineteen, he was a crewman on a flatboat carrying cargo down the Mississippi River to New Orleans. One evening, when the boat was tied up at the riverbank for the night, it was boarded by seven runaway blacks, armed and out for blood and plunder. Lincoln and the rest of the crew repulsed the invaders, cut the boat's hawser and drifted out of reach. At the end of that voyage, however, young Abe got his first look at a slave auction, in the New Orleans marketplace—husbands being sold separately from their wives, mothers from their children, all to be sundered forever. The sight aroused his pity and anger, and for the rest of his life he harbored an intense hatred of slaveholding. He once told a White House visitor, "Whenever I hear anyone arguing for slavery, I feel a strong impulse to see it tried on him personally."

Lincoln was a writer as well as a speaker and a doer. And, since generally we can find a truer image of a writer in his writings than in his deeds and spoken words, so do we perceive in Lincoln's handwritten letters, notes and speech drafts the true gentle-man. His first school composition was an essay on cruelty to animals; he wrote angrily of his schoolmates' catching turtles and putting hot coals on their shells to make the poor creatures try to run. In Lincoln's letters written during his struggling days in Springfield, we glimpse his frustration: "I am quite as lonesome here as I ever was anywhere in my life. I have been spoken to by but one woman since I've been here, and should not have been by her if she could have avoided it." Then there was this circular he wrote and handed around during his first (and unsuccessful) campaign for the state legislature: "Every man is said to have his ambition. I can say that I have no other so great as that of being truly esteemed of my fellow men, by rendering myself worthy of their esteem."

The words Lincoln wrote and spoke while in the White House are too well known to need repeating. Perhaps his most quoted expression is the one he employed to define the North's postwar policy toward the South: "With malice toward none; with charity for all . . ." His Gettysburg Address, scribbled out in fragmentary notes while he was riding a train to the dedication of the battlefield as a National Cemetery, is probably the most eloquent use of words (just 263 words) in any American historical document. As for the words of others *about* Lincoln, even his opponents and detractors grudgingly had to grant his virtues, while his admirers said such things as, "There is no man in the country so wise, so gentle and so firm," and, at his deathbed, "Now he belongs to the ages." The ages have only carved deeper his niche in history's hall of fame, and confirmed to later generations that here, in truth, was a gentle-man.

FATHER DAMIEN

At the time of Lincoln's death, another man, destined also to be a gentle hero, had just been ordained a priest in Honolulu, Hawaii. In his native Belgium, his name had been Joseph de Veuster. Sent as a missionary to the South Seas, he was twenty-five when he was elevated to the priesthood, and took the name "Father Damien." He worked for a number of years on various Pacific islands. He returned to Hawaii in 1873 to attend the dedication of a new chapel, however, and after the ceremony he got into conversation with the bishop, who was worried because he could not find a permanent missionary for the colony of Kalaupapa on the neighboring island of Molokai. Only an occasional priest would serve there, and then only briefly. There was good reason for a man to refuse to stay long at Kalaupapa. This was a peninsula walled about by mountains, safely apart from the rest of Molokai—apart from the rest of Hawaii, and the rest of the world, for that matter. It was the settlement in which all the Hawaiian islands' lepers were confined—a concentration camp, really—where they could not infect others.

From time immemorial, the dread disease of leprosy has terrified mankind more than any other. The unfortunates afflicted with it were literally "the untouchables." During the Middle Ages, lepers were commanded to carry and tinkle a little bell wherever they went, to warn healthy folk out of their way. In many places, anyone from an infant to an oldster who showed the first symptom of leprosy— usually a patch of skin that became insensitive even to severe pain-producing stimuli—was hustled off to live out his life in the company of other lepers. And their lives could be long and dreadful, the horrible devastation of the disease often taking years to rot them to death.

Today we know that leprosy can be cured if diagnosed early, and that even in the latter stages its ravages can be arrested. We also know that the chance of a healthy person's catching the disease from a leper is very small, except after prolonged and intimate contact. In Father Damien's day, however, leprosy still held all the terrors and superstitions that had repelled people throughout history. Mercifully, Hawaii did provision the colony at Kalaupapa, but the supplies were meager and infrequent, and the boatmen hastily unloaded them at a deserted beach, to which the poor cripples had to struggle to fetch them. Thus it was a moment of true and unselfish heroism when—as soon as the bishop had outlined the situation—Father Damien volunteered to be the permanent priest to the unfortunates at Kalaupapa. He set out that very day by boat to Molokai island, and was not to leave it again for sixteen years, and then by the one exit available to the lepers.

Father Damien found his new parishioners living in squalor. There was no hospital nor decent housing; the government wouldn't send building materials. There was no medical attention; doctors and nurses wouldn't visit, and the authorities wouldn't send even the simplest medicines. The lepers lived in self-built huts of palm leaves. Father Damien was appalled to find them as full of vice as of disease.

They considered themselves "the living dead," so why should they care how foully they sinned? They passed their time by engaging in immoral sexual acts or else drinking themselves into forgetfulness on beer they fermented from *ki* roots.

Father Damien realized he could not change their sordid life by preaching platitudes about morality, nor by preaching a hope that he knew would be false. Instead, he set about improving their living conditions (*his* only "house" was a palm tree under which he slept). Sending a ceaseless series of messages to Honolulu, he bullied the authorities into one concession after another. They sent building materials, and Father Damien and the healthier colonists erected a hospital for the worst cases. He demanded and got medicines. There was nothing in those days that would alleviate the leprosy, of course, but he was able to treat the commoner ailments that afflict lepers as well as other people. He got more building materials, and replaced the colonists' miserable huts with neat cottages.

The colony had been a pigsty when he came. That was when Father Damien took up smoking for the first time in his life: a pipe of

tobacco so bitter that its smoke masked the stench of the lepers. They lived in filth, and seldom bathed, because their only source of water was a scummy pool so far away that few of them could make the arduous round trip with a bucket. Father Damien found a crystalline clear pool in a high valley, and again bullied Honolulu until he got a boatload of water pipe. Then he and his helpers laid a pipeline from the pond that brought running water to the colony for the first time. His labors soon had the effect he had hoped for. The colonists became ashamed of their former bad habits, and their morals rose along with their spirits. They helped Father Damien build a small church, and began to attend it regularly. The good priest also persuaded teachers to come from "outside"—only briefly, to be sure, but long enough to teach the lepers reading and writing, along with some simple arts and crafts. Eventually, the colonists were producing little souvenir items for sale (after thorough fumigation) to the other islanders and to tourists. With the money earned, they bought further small comforts for themselves. They were still dying, but they were no longer "the living dead." They were a part of the world again!

Then, one day while preparing a meal, Father Damien chanced to spill a pot of scalding water on his bare foot. He felt it not at all. When next he preached to his congregation, he did not, as before, refer to "my brethren." He said, "We lepers . . ."

He was hardly surprised that he had contracted leprosy. After all, he had lived among these lepers for years, dressing sores in the hospital, washing the bodies of those too weak to care for themselves, praying beside their deathbeds, even digging their graves. And he had known the risk, from that day he boarded the Molokai boat. (Joseph de Veuster had been a handsome man, with black curly hair and beard, a smiling mouth, a short, straight nose.) After sixteen years on the island, at forty-nine, Father Damien had a forehead bulging over his eyes, skin tight, silver-gray and unnaturally glossy. His eyebrows were gone, his nose sunken in, his ears greatly enlarged. His hands and face were covered with lumps like boils.

In April of 1889, bedridden, wasted, blind, deaf and almost unable to talk, he mumbled thickly, "The work of the lepers is assured, and I am no longer necessary, and so will go up yonder." Thus he left Kalaupapa—or his soul did—the only way a leper could leave. But the world had heard of his labors, had learned that lepers could live decently, work usefully and endure their slow doom stoically, even cheerfully. Other volunteers in other countries took up Father

Damien's work, and applied his methods, to the great benefit of lepers all over the world. One gentle hero had quelled the terror and superstition of countless centuries.

MAHATMA GANDHI

Since a gentle hero is one who does his heroics quietly and without fanfare, there could hardly ever have been a gentler hero than Mohandas Gandhi, who accomplished notable deeds by deliberately doing virtually nothing. That makes him sound like a zero rather than a hero, but such was not the case.

Mohandas K. Gandhi was born in India in 1869. He was a short, spindly, frail little chap with jug ears, and, possibly because he cut such a poor figure, he was painfully shy. He uncomplainingly let his parents marry him to a girl he had never seen before their wedding. (They were each thirteen years old!) He uncomplainingly let himself be packed off to England for education as a lawyer. Possibly as his one gesture of independence, he set up practice not in India but in South Africa. Because of his shyness, the first case he took to court was his last. When it came his turn to address the court, he was struck speechless, fled from the courtroom, and forthwith abandoned the practice of law.

However, in his quiet way, Gandhi was already doing heroic things. In 1899, he joined in the South African War then going on between the English and Dutch. His intentions were to help, however, and not to hurt. He helped raise and later commanded an ambulance and field hospital unit. Later, when an epidemic broke out in Johannesburg, he organized a plague hospital. By now, he had overcome his shame at having failed at law and had somewhat conquered his shyness. Enough, anyway, to dare to joust with the dragon of injustice.

In the early 1900's, the European population of South Africa resented the multitude of Indians who had emigrated there and, once there, through industry and good business sense had prospered rather better than most of the "whites." (The South Africans of English and Dutch descent considered themselves to be the only "whites"— although Indians are really of the same Caucasian race—and sneeringly called the Indians "wogs" and worse.) The Indians were second-class citizens, persecuted and oppressed. Mohandas Gandhi determined to boost the status of his people by a tactic he called *Satyagraha,* which can be translated as "passive resistance" or "non-violent non-cooperation." Indians were forbidden to ride in the first-class sections of South African trains; so, on Gandhi's instructions, they simply stopped riding trains. They were allowed to put up only at the grubbiest hotels, so they stopped patronizing hotels altogether. Their own shops and businesses were harshly regulated by all manner of unfair laws, rules and red tape; so they simply stopped doing business.

In a short time, the "whites" realized that it was no longer the "wogs" who were hurting; it was themselves. All of South Africa's economy was grinding to a standstill. Eventually, Gandhi's policy of *Satyagraha* wrung from the government new laws forbidding discrimination and upgrading the Indians to equal standing with all other citizens of the country. The grateful and admiring Indians gave Gandhi the title of *Mahatma* ("Great Soul"), and he divested himself of everything European—including his clothing. For the rest of his life, he wore nothing but a simple loincloth and a shawl.

Now Gandhi went to India to see if his policy of *Satyagraha* could succeed in securing his homeland's independence. India had been a British colony since the eighteenth century, and had tried everything from diplomatic haggling to repeated insurrections to get free of the Empire. Gandhi came home a hero, his exploits in South Africa well known, and he had no trouble in arranging acts of *Satyagraha* "non-cooperation" in several cities. However, many of his followers were ignorant, uncontrollable hotheads from the back country. These soon became impatient with passive resistance and broke loose in bloody riots. The British colonial authorities held Gandhi responsible, and jailed him. This happened time after time: the non-violent campaigns would turn into mob mutinies,' and Gandhi would be imprisoned for them. Even the authorities knew he had nothing to do with the riots, but part of Gandhi's philosophy was that he was responsible for anything his followers might do, and so he took the punishment on their behalf. He once said, "Non-violence is the first article of my faith. It is also the last article."

Gandhi was seldom in prison for long, however, for he developed another effective tactic. Whenever he disapproved of any action by the British, he started a "fast unto death," stubbornly refusing any nourishment except an occasional sip of water. Actually, this wasn't any great hardship for the Mahatma; all his life he had been a Hindu vegetarian, living on little but fruit and nuts. However, his fasts frightened the colonial authorities; they knew that if ever he did starve to death, the Indian people would regard him as a martyr to

British cruelty and the whole subcontinent would explode in rebellion. So, when Gandhi fasted, the officials eventually gave in to him: set him free from jail, corrected whatever abuse he was protesting, or acceded to whatever demand he made.

Mahatma Gandhi was by now India's national hero; Great Britain ruled in name only. By the time the Second World War broke out, Britain could no longer count on recruiting Indian volunteer troops, as it always had in earlier days. (In fact, a sizable "Indian national army" marched off to fight for the Japanese.) In 1942, Gandhi made his offer: India would join in the war on Britain's side if independence were immediately granted. Britain indignantly refused, and deemed Gandhi so impertinent that this time he was jailed for two years, fasts or no fasts.

In its own good time, and for its own good reasons (mainly that India had become more of a troublesome liability than an asset), Britain set India free in 1947. But the terms of independence were not dictated by Mahatma Mohandas Gandhi. The Indian subcontinent has always had numerous conflicting religions, with the Hindu and Moslem being the most prominent, and there had always been strife among the true believers. Although Gandhi was by birth a Hindu, he had hoped that an independent India could influence all its varied religions to live in peace. However, the leader of the Moslem faction, Mahomed Ali Jinnah, was inflexible; he demanded of the British that the subcontinent should be divided along religious lines. The British listened to Jinnah. The land would henceforth be divided into two countries: Hindu India and Moslem Pakistan. Gandhi was grieved but, for the sake of the long-wanted independence, he reluctantly agreed to the partition.

No sooner had independence been declared in August of 1947 than the two new nations erupted in religious war. Hindus residing in Moslem Pakistan were butchered. Moslems in Hindu India were butchered. Between August and the end of the year, some half million people died; it was the bloodiest "holy war" in history. There was nothing Gandhi could do to stop the slaughter . . . except sit in his garden, surrounded by his followers, and lead them in prayer. Outside that garden, however, there were many who blamed Gandhi's passivity for the whole mess. One young Hindu came into Gandhi's garden on January 30, 1948, bowed before the old man, received the Mahatma's blessing, then drew a pistol and shot the Great Soul dead.

It may seem odd, but by "doing nothing," simply sitting there and

being shot, Gandhi stopped the war. Hindus and Moslems alike revered him. The news of his death seemed suddenly to make them
realize that bloodshed was the last thing the Mahatma would have
wanted of them. There was immediate peace between India and
Pakistan, between Hindus and Moslems. (There have been flare-
ups in the years since, but none to compare with that post-indepen-
dence bloodbath.) Of the peace-loving Gandhi's death by violence,
which brought the peace, a biographer has written, "There could
have been no better end for a life that was all devotion, all sacrifice . . . all love."

ALBERT SCHWEITZER

Ask almost anyone what he or she is doing about the pressing
problems of today—ecological decay, the population explosion, the
arms race, even petty corruption in city hall? The reply is likely to
be a shrugged "What can one person do?"

Well, Albert Schweitzer was one person. He could have had an
outstanding career in his native Germany in any of several fields.
Before he was out of his thirties, he had a solid reputation as a the-
ologist (he wrote several books on religion); as a philosopher (he
wrote books on that subject, too); and as a master musician (he was
a superb organist, the world's best interpreter of the music of Jo-
hann Sebastian Bach, and the author of the definitive book on Bach's
life and work). All these accomplishments and bright prospects young
Schweitzer left behind, to spend his life in one of the most remote
spots on earth, helping people that the rest of the world had hardly heard of.

Two things influenced his decision. He was principal of a Protestant seminary when he began to develop ideas of his own about
Christianity; ideas that differed considerably from what he was expected to teach his student ministers. For one, he believed that a
man should do good in this world, but he shouldn't do it just to get
into heaven or to stay out of hell. He should do it because of his
"reverence for life." Schweitzer resigned from the seminary: "I decided I would have my life and work say what I believed." Also, he
suffered a serious illness that required two painful operations. He
then declared: "One who has been delivered from pain is now a man
whose eyes are open to pain and anguish, and he must help to bring
to others the deliverance which he has himself enjoyed." So Schweitzer studied medicine, and became Herr Doktor Schweitzer. But he

did not settle down to an easy and profitable practice in Germany. In 1913, he went to where there was precious little ease and certainly no profits—to Africa and to Gabon, a country that straddles the equator—and there, at a village called Lambaréné, he began treating the native blacks.

Schweitzer was sent by no church mission, supported by no foundation. He personally paid for the erection of his clinic's first buildings with the earnings from his book on Bach. There were many who thought him crazy. A high proportion of Africa's millions were diseased, crippled or afflicted in some way. In Gabon alone, one native in sixty was a leper, and almost all the rest were ailing with such diseases as malaria and dysentery. It would take thousands of doctors to make even a dent in the death rate or in the disease statistics. True, agreed Schweitzer, but "a single doctor in Africa, even with the most modest equipment, can in a single year free hundreds of men from the grip of suffering and death." That might go unnoticed in the immensity of Africa, but it was what one person could do, and, indeed, it was much more than most ever do.

Schweitzer never again left Lambaréné, except for brief visits to Europe and America to seek donations of funds and medical supplies to keep his clinic going. He stayed there, in that sweltering, hot, humid equatorial climate, living just as the Africans did. He never aspired to build a towering, shining white hospital; the primitive natives would have been afraid of such a thing. Instead, his clinic remained a simple African village of wooden huts and mud streets full of pigs, chickens and goats. Only the operating room had a generator-powered electric light. All the other buildings were lighted with candles or kerosene lamps. The patients ranged from pygmies to cannibals. And their doctor, the man who had once recorded Bach's magnificent music on the mightiest church organs of Europe, now played hymns each Sunday on a tinny, out-of-tune piano decayed by jungle dampness and heat.

When a patient came to Lambaréné, often from miles and miles away, he brought his whole family. They were all assigned to a hut, and lived together while the patient was treated—cooking their own meals and earning their keep by helping clean around the compound, dispose of garbage, etc. Dr. Schweitzer treated all those too poor to pay, but insisted on a token payment whenever a patient could afford it, because he knew his patients would be more respectful of his treatment if it cost something. (The average payment was less than twenty-five cents, for anything from malaria pills to major surgery.) However, even after his patients had come to trust the doctor and believe in his cures, Schweitzer still had to contend with the African witch doctors, who resented his presence and often threatened to lay a curse on anyone who visited the clinic.

Schweitzer also had to contend with the jungle. Steadily, since 1913, his workers had to keep hacking at it just to maintain a clearing for the clinic compound. Leave the jungle alone for as little as two months and it would overgrow and obliterate all of Lambaréné. And there were the jungle hazards: leopards, cobras, pythons, crocodiles, mosquitoes carrying malaria and yellow fever, tsetse flies carrying the sleeping sickness, termites that ate and undermined the clinic buildings, ants that ate food stores and medicines.

Schweitzer was not "one person" for long. Although he was averse to publicity or praise, word of his undertaking spread through Africa and the world. Other doctors, nurses and just plain people who wanted to help asked to join him. Schweitzer screened them carefully; the jungle is no place for weaklings or incompetents. But eventually he had a sizable and efficient staff of surgeons, physicians, nurses, cooks, carpenters, mechanics. From all over the world came donations, large and small, of supplies, drugs, money. Schweitzer, in showing what one person could do, had lighted a candle in the middle of darkest Africa that found a kindred glint in men's souls everywhere.

Albert Schweitzer died in 1965, at Lambaréné, where he had spent two-thirds of his life. He was vigorous, active, and still practicing medicine to the last. One of the last times he left Lambaréné was in 1957, to go to Sweden to accept the Nobel Peace Prize. The prize, in addition to being one of the world's most distinguished honors, included an award of many thousands of dollars; enough to have enabled Schweitzer to live in comparative luxury for the rest of his life. Instead, he used every cent of the money to build—a little way from the Lambaréné clinic—an entire village for his leper patients. Lambaréné still thrives under the men Schweitzer taught, and still stands as a symbol of what one person can do. We, and everyone, might well remember a few words from Albert Schweitzer's Nobel Prize acceptance speech: "You don't live in a world all alone. Your brothers are here too."

Against All Odds

But the bravest are surely those who have
the clearest vision of what is before them, glory
and danger alike, and yet go out to meet it.

—Thucydides

Ludwig van Beethoven

Ludwig van Beethoven was Germany's foremost composer; perhaps the greatest of all composers. But in his life he had to surmount a veritable mountain of handicaps. In his youth, he was often impoverished; while living in a drafty garret he caught a cold which developed into an ear infection that he never could cure. Despite that and other afflictions—a crushing disappointment in love, constant money worries, nagging family quarrels—he managed to create such masterworks as his first eight symphonies. Beethoven's Fifth Symphony is probably the world's best known and oftenest played symphony, though his Third ("Eroica") and Sixth ("Pastoral") are not far behind. He also composed piano concertos, including the famous Fifth ("Emperor"); violin sonatas, including the famous Ninth ("Kreutzer"); countless other orchestral and chamber works, and an opera, *Fidelio.*

Then, of all the terrible things that can happen to a musician, about the worst happened to Beethoven. In 1818 his old ear infection worsened, and he became totally deaf. It seems incredible that a composer could write notes and chords and harmonies that he could never hear—and that some of the most splendid music ever written—but Beethoven continued his work. His output in this period included his masterpiece of masterpieces, the Ninth ("Chorale") Symphony, a work as yet unsurpassed and probably unsurpassable. When he attended the premiere performance, he sat watching an orchestra that to him was playing in silence. And when the symphony concluded—with the audience applauding wildly—poor Beethoven had to be turned around in his chair to see the people standing in homage, clapping their hands, weeping, cheering.

Edgar Allan Poe

The American writer Edgar Allan Poe had always to struggle against poverty, and, like Beethoven, he also had to fight a crippling affliction. His whole life long, he suffered from the disease of alcoholism. He published his first book of poems at the age of eighteen, in 1827, and this earned him a prestigious job as editor of a popular magazine; but his drinking cost him that job—and another and an-

other. Poe was too proud and confident of his talent to let himself slip entirely into the gutter. In order to write at all, he had to wage a terrible and heroic inner battle against the urge to drink, but he did manage to do this for short intervals, and turned out the haunting stories and poems that have been famous ever since; perhaps it was his internal torment that made him the master of grotesque and weird tales. He is also acknowledged to have been the "father" of the mystery story. In American literature, he is ranked with Nathaniel Hawthorne and Herman Melville; he might have reached the stature of Mark Twain and even greater writers had he lived long enough. But his battle with the bottle was a losing one.

When, in 1836, he married his teen-age cousin, Virginia Clemm, he managed to stay sober for long periods at a time, because she was fatally ill with tuberculosis, and required his almost constant attention. Attention was about all he could give her, for, no matter how hard he worked or how popular his stories, his tightfisted publishers simply never paid him enough to live on. One of the most poignant 47, when Edgar and Virginia occupied an unheated cottage in a episodes in literary history occurred during the cruel winter of 1846- New York City suburb. Poe could do nothing for his dying wife but sit by her bedside and—since they could not afford blankets—try to keep her warm by covering her with his old overcoat and setting the family cat on her laboring breast. She died before the winter was out, and from then on Poe's life was all downhill.

In 1849, he was in Baltimore, where a city election was in progress. In those days, a politician would round up all the skid-row derelicts and send them from one polling booth to another, where they'd register each time under a different name, and would give them a stiff drink for each vote they cast for him. Edgar Allan Poe was among this bunch of derelicts, and at nightfall a friend found him sodden and unconscious in the street; he had reached the gutter at last. The intake of alcohol had evidently burst a blood vessel in what had been the brain of a genius. Though the friend rushed him to a hospital, Poe died in delirium, at the age of forty.

Vincent Van Gogh

Another genius who fought against odds to do the work he felt he had to do was the Dutch painter Vincent Van Gogh. He, too, was dogged by poverty, and by a touch of insanity which made him alternately brooding and frenzied. His brutally honest self-portraits show an unnatural melancholy in his eyes and an oddly misshapen skull; it is possible that he suffered from some pressure on his brain. Although he lived in an age (the late 1880's) when artists were experimenting with all kinds of "new ways of seeing," even his fellow artists could not properly appreciate Van Gogh's "barbaric colors, intense emotion and hatchet-stroke style." In fact, Van Gogh sold just one painting in his whole lifetime, and that was for only a few hundred francs. Still, he kept on working. He would often go without food to buy paints, and when he couldn't afford them, he would grind his own pigments from earth colors. He would have starved but for his younger brother Theo, who gave him occasional driblets of money, and, though a mere businessman, was the only human being who had faith in Vincent's work.

In his last years, when he was living in the south of France, Van Gogh's long-smoldering insanity erupted in violence. He threatened his painter friend, Paul Gauguin, with a knife—and then, in a fit of remorse, sliced off his own ear. He was committed to an asylum. After a period of treatment, he began to enjoy lucid intervals during which the doctors let him out of the asylum to paint in the countryside. Here he did some of his best work. Among the pictures he painted at this time was "Cornfield with Crows." Showing a flock of black and ominous birds settling from a threatening sky onto a quiet and sunlit field, this is a veritable illustration of Van Gogh's mental condition. Finally he could stand it no longer and, in 1890 at the age of thirty-seven, he shot himself. Today, Van Gogh's paintings are proudly displayed in the world's leading museums and their total value is high in the millions of dollars. Van Gogh had sold just the one, but he knew his worth, and his lonely fight to express himself is, by any definition, heroism.

GALILEO GALILEI

Many other men and women besides artists, writers and musicians have had to buck disheartening odds, including—besides poverty and mental or physical affliction—superstition, narrow-minded authority, racial prejudice, or just the fate of being "too far ahead of their time."

For instance, one of history's towering scientific geniuses suffered much at the hands of the Church. His name was Galileo Galilei, and he was born in 1564, by which time the Reformation had divided the monolithic Church of the Middle Ages. In Italy the Roman Catholic Church still held sway, and still held to its conviction that faith should not be challenged by reason. Galileo invented the world's first astronomical telescope. He also laid the foundations for modern experimental science. He *demonstrated* what people otherwise would have refused to believe. For example, could anyone believe that a heavy iron ball would fall through space no faster than a light wooden ball? Galileo proved, by dropping such different weights from the Leaning Tower of Pisa, that both would reach the ground at the same instant.

The Church was not unduly perturbed by Galileo's experiments and the truths they proved, until he turned his telescope to the skies. Nicholas Copernicus had recently shown, by mathematical proofs, that the earth was only one small planet in a planetary system revolving around the sun. This the Church could not accept. Since man was "created in God's image," then obviously, man's earth had to be the center of the universe. The Church knew, however, that the commonfolk were not likely to understand Copernicus' complicated arithmetic. Galileo looked at the heavens and saw that Copernicus' theories were true. He invited others to look through the telescope, too, and see for themselves. This was a different matter and did provoke the Church. Galileo was summoned to Rome and put on trial. In his defense, he offered proof of his findings. He invited the Church inquisitors to look through his telescope and see some of the interesting things he had seen—for instance, that the sun has blemishes (sun spots). The inquisitors scoffed; nothing in God's universe could be blemished; Galileo obviously had dust spots on his lenses. Well then, begged Galileo, look at the moons he had discovered orbiting the planet Jupiter. The inquisitors said haughtily that Jupiter had no moons, or certainly the ancient sages would have mentioned them.

The trial ended with the inquisitors offering Galileo the choice of either freely disowning all his discoveries and stopping the publishing of them or be tortured until he did recant. The threat was sufficient to make the old man kneel, repent of his "heresies" and promise to go and sin no more. He did keep silent thereafter, but he continued his experiments in secret, making several other important astronomical discoveries. Even after increasing age brought blindness, Galileo continued to work—for one thing, discovering how to use the motion of a pendulum to make the world's first accurate clock (which another inventor built after his death). Galileo died in 1642. In defiance of the all-powerful Church, he had kept notes of all his theories, inventions and discoveries. These were smuggled out of

Catholic Italy and published in the Protestant Netherlands, and thus were preserved for the inspiration of all the generations of scientists since.

The color of a man's skin has often been a fearsome obstacle to his ambition, and the overcoming of that obstacle has often been heroic. When Jack Johnson became the first black ever to win the heavy-weight boxing championship of the world, by defeating Tommy Burns in 1908, white "sportsmen" refused to recognize his championship until he agreed to win it all over again. A former white champion, the most formidable fighter of his time, Jim Jeffries, was persuaded to come out of retirement and teach this upstart Negro a lesson. John-son won the fight easily and had to be recognized as the champion, but there began an immediate and frantic search for a "white hope" to knock the crown off that black head. One after another, white boxers were sent against Johnson, but he defeated them all and held the championship until 1915, when Jess Willard won it back "for the whites." But not for good. Since that time, many Negroes have lit-erally fought their way to fame—because, until very recent times, there were only two fields in which a black American could make a mark: in the boxing ring and in show business.

It was not until 1947 that a Negro broke the color barrier in major league baseball, when Jackie Robinson was signed by the Brooklyn Dodgers. Now there are black stars on the baseball teams, as well as in football, basketball, tennis, golf and just about any other sport you can name. An Australian aborigine girl, Evonne Goolagong—of the one black race that has been oppressed and discriminated against more cruelly than any other—has lately become a shining star of the international tennis circuit. Still, the odds have not at all shifted in favor of the blacks. As recently as 1973, when the home-run record of Negro batting ace Hank Aaron began to creep up on the number of home runs (714) hit by the legendary Babe Ruth in his lifetime career, Aaron was deluged with hate mail from white bigots, threatening all kinds of revenge if he should dare to break Ruth's record. Undaunted, Aaron proceeded to do just that in 1974 and, at this writing, is still hitting home runs.

JIM THORPE

You don't have to wear a black skin to have the odds stacked against you; a red skin will do. Jim Thorpe, now acknowledged as the greatest all-around athlete known to sports history, was greeted with scorn and sneers at the beginning of his career because his original name had been Bright Path and his mother was a Sac Indian squaw. The Carlisle Indian School, founded in 1879 as the first non-reservation school of higher education for Indians, had never been heard of by most white Americans until Jim Thorpe enrolled there and led the obscure Carlisle football team to unbelievable upset victories over such "unbeatable" opponents as Harvard, Army and the University of Pennsylvania.

The ordinary football player is about as adept at any less rugged sport as a gorilla is at chess. But Jim Thorpe went from college into the 1912 Olympics, held in Stockholm, Sweden. Though he was pitted against highly (and expensively) trained athletes from all over the world, and though he had never been able to afford coaching in any of the Olympic sports, Thorpe was the star of the Games. He finished first in three events of the pentathlon (the broad jump, the 200-meter run and the 1,500-meter run) and was second in the other two events; thus he swept the pentathlon with a score twice that of his nearest rival. He placed first in three events of the decathlon (the shot put, the 1,500-meter run and the hurdle race) and was second in every one of the seven other events; thus winning the decathlon as well. Sweden's King Gustav V was so impressed that he gave the big Indian a special jeweled trophy in the shape of a Viking ship.

"You, sir," said King Gustav at the presentation, "are the greatest athlete in the world." Jim Thorpe made what is probably the least flowery acceptance speech in the history of athletics. He said, "Thanks, King."

Only amateurs and not paid professionals, however, are allowed to compete in the Olympics. And two years before, Thorpe had been a meagerly paid player for a backwoods North Carolina baseball team, not realizing that this would have repercussions. When that fact was discovered, Thorpe was stripped of all his medals and trophies. Search though you may through the archives of the Olympic Games, you will find not the slightest mention of Jim Thorpe or the still-unbroken records he set. That does not diminish his stature in the least. Thorpe would rank as a sports immortal if he had done nothing but play football. In more than thirty college football games, he never once took a "time out," but played every one of the sixty minutes of each game. In one season, he scored twenty-five touchdowns and 198 points, a record still unmatched by any other player. After the Olympics fiasco, he became a baseball player for the New

York Giants, then the Boston Braves, and then shifted to professional football, where he played until he was forty. He died in 1953, but he is still remembered in the National Football League's "Jim Thorpe Trophy," awarded annually, the most coveted honor any pro player can receive. And in 1954 his hometown of Mauch Chunk, Pa., changed its name to Jim Thorpe in his honor.

Let us turn now to a very different saga of heroism. One that spans 139 years and interconnects the lives of three almost super-human women. All of them, at first acquaintance, would have seemed *sub*human, so cruelly handicapped were they—yet each in turn, helped by the one before her, overcame odds that would have staggered Herakles.

Laura Bridgman

The first of the three, Laura Bridgman, was born in New Hampshire in 1829. At the age of two, she was stricken by scarlet fever, which left her both blind and deaf. This meant she was doomed never to see the world's beauty, never to hear the world's sounds, never to communicate with another human being—and, even worse, never to learn anything, not even to feed or dress herself. Consider this: the way a person learns is by watching, listening and reading; Laura could do none of these. It is possible to teach a blind person to read books (printed in Braille) because the blind student can hear the teacher. It is possible to teach a deaf person, because the student can see the teacher and can read books. Even a deaf person who has never heard words can be taught to talk, because the teacher can demonstrate lip and tongue and breathing movements. But for a person both blind and deaf, practically from birth, there is no avenue of communication—or so it was thought at the time.

In the very year of her birth, however, there was started in Massachusetts the Perkins Institution, whose director, Dr. Samuel Howe, was determined to try to teach such "unteachables." Laura was enrolled at the age of eight. No one would ever have guessed that Laura was an exceptionally bright child. Dr. Howe taught her the names of common articles—spoon, knife, fork, and so on—by pasting labels on them with the names in raised letters that she could feel. This took a long time, but from there it was only a short step to learning the individual letters, the whole alphabet and the ten numerical digits. Another little while and she understood that the letters and digits could be put together, rearranged, put together again

—to impart the whole of human knowledge. By the age of fourteen, she had learned a manual alphabet, so she could "talk" to her teachers by touch, and was deep in the study of geography and astronomy —the world and the stars she would never see. Just as surprisingly, she became an expert seamstress and decided never to leave the school, but to live there (until she died in 1889) and be the school's sewing teacher.

Anne Sullivan

In 1876, a little ten-year-old blind girl, an orphan named Anne Sullivan, was admitted to the school. She had gone blind only gradually, and her hearing and speech were perfect, so her training was not so difficult as that of others in the institution. One of her favorite teachers was Laura Bridgman, so Anne learned the manual alphabet in order to be able to converse with her. In time, a series of operations gave Anne Sullivan back her sight, and she left the school. Having been handicapped herself and having learned from the Perkins Institution—especially from Laura Bridgman—that the handicapped could be helped, she went to work as a private tutor to help other handicapped children. In the course of her work, she became acquainted with Alexander Graham Bell, who had previously headed a school for the deaf (and whose experiments in the transmission of sound had led him to invent the telephone).

Helen Keller

Meanwhile, in 1880, a girl named Helen Keller had been born in Alabama and, like Laura Bridgman, had been stricken in infancy with a fever that left her blind and deaf (and mute, as a consequence of the deafness). By the age of six, she was like a ferocious wild animal. Laura Bridgman had been an intelligent and patient child; Helen Keller had more than intelligence, however; she had genius inside her—it raged to be let out of the darkness and the silence. Her parents, unable to cope with her, appealed to the famous Dr. Bell for advice on how she might be educated—or at least tamed. Dr. Bell sent them Anne Sullivan.

What Laura Bridgman had learned with such difficulty and passed along so patiently to Anne Sullivan, Miss Sullivan now undertook to teach to this savage child, so pitiable in her predicament, so detestable in her behavior. Mr. and Mrs. Keller had let "the poor thing" have her way; Anne Sullivan didn't. She was strict, even severe in quelling Helen's tantrums. And Helen was so quick of mind that when she realized she was being treated as a spoiled brat, she also realized that she was being treated—for the first time—as a human being. Within a matter of days she respected Anne Sullivan, within a matter of weeks she began learning from her, within a month she knew the manual alphabet.

She learned her first word when Anne held her hand under a running faucet, while tracing the word's letters in her palm. "I knew then," Helen Keller wrote, years later, "that w-a-t-e-r meant the wonderful cool something that was flowing over my hand. That living

word awakened my soul, gave it light, hope, joy, set it free! Everything had a name, and each name gave birth to a new thought."

When Anne had taught Helen all she could, she accompanied her to schools for the deaf in Boston and New York for more advanced studies. Helen learned to read and write (Braille) and to speak. In 1900 she entered Radcliffe College and graduated with honors in 1908. Unlike Laura Bridgman, who had elected to live in safe seclusion at the Perkins school and help individual students as best she could, Helen Keller was bold enough to strike out into the wide world, to prove that the "unteachable" could be taught, to raise funds for teaching them, and to champion other social causes. With Anne Sullivan as her guiding eyes (and, after Anne's death in 1936, with Polly Thompson for companion), Helen traveled and lectured all over America, in Europe and Asia. She learned several languages, and studied in many fields of learning. She wrote eight books, on varying topics, but all attesting to one thing: that the most terribly handicapped human being is still a human being, and can be a happy and useful one.

Helen Keller died in 1968, but long before that her example had inspired many others to take up her cause, more schools to be opened to the handicapped, and many more "unteachables" to become, as she had, a vital part of the world. Helen Keller couldn't have done it without Anne Sullivan, nor could Anne have done it without Laura Bridgman. The history of these three heroic women spanning 139 years is certainly one of success against all odds.

Franklin D. Roosevelt

Helen Keller once sent a letter of encouragement to a man she didn't know—but who was later to become a friend and admirer—at a time when that man really needed encouraging. At the age of thirty-nine, he had already enjoyed considerable success, and had a promising future ahead of him. He had come from a wealthy family, attended the best schools, practiced as a lawyer, been elected to the New York Senate, been appointed by President Woodrow Wilson as Assistant Secretary of the Navy and served with distinction from 1913 through the First World War and until 1920. In that year he had been selected to run for Vice President on the ticket with Presidential hopeful James M. Cox. Though Cox lost to Warren Harding, it had meant only a temporary setback for his running partner. This man was a comer. His name was Franklin Delano Roosevelt.

And then, in 1921, he was stricken with polio. He nearly died, and, after he had passed the crisis point, he almost wished he had. For he would never walk again. He had apparently been stopped cold in mid-career by what he called "this damned children's disease." His domineering mother insisted that he retire from public life and lead the empty, useless existence of a country squire on the family estate. But his wife, Eleanor, knew that kind of life would turn Franklin into a husk of a man. She, along with his closest friends and scores of well-wishers like Helen Keller, urged him to dare the odds and go on serving his country.

It was a long, hard climb back to health for what remained of his living body. His legs were to be nothing but dead weights for the rest of his life. He was never what you could call cheerful about his disability. But nevertheless he learned how to get about, wearing rigid braces and leaning on heavy canes. And he swung back into political campaigning—literally "swung" on those canes—and was elected Governor of New York in 1928, again in 1930, and in 1932 became the thirty-second President of the United States. He was probably the most popular President the nation has ever had; the only one ever elected to four terms in office. (The two-term tradition was suspended by the immediate threat of another World War; no one wanted to "change horses in midstream.")

Among Roosevelt's achievements, he led the United States out of the Great Depression of the 1930's, and victoriously through the worst war the world has known. He instituted the "good neighbor policy" with the other countries of the Americas. He initiated Social Security for the support of the elderly. He was one of the founding fathers of the United Nations. He once said, perhaps ironically but not bitterly, that he was able to get so much done because, unlike other people, he had only half a body to worry about. He did all these things and many more, while—surprising though this may sound—concealing from many people that he was handicapped at all.

He avoided stairways, none of which he could climb. He always entered his limousine and railroad car out of sight of the public, because he had so much trouble getting into them. He had himself secretly carried beforehand onto any platform where he was to speak. Although in private he used a wheelchair, in public he was always on his feet (inconspicuously propped up by a couple of aides standing behind him). Cameramen were courteous enough to photograph him only from the waist up. To the day of his death in 1945, there were numerous Americans (and even emissaries of other governments who had visited him) who never realized that he was disabled. Franklin D. Roosevelt is the only "legless" man in history to become head of state. He had beaten the odds far beyond all expectations. He had lived not just a useful life but a necessary one; looking back, it is hard to see how the American people at that period could have gotten along without him.

DOUGLAS BADER

Of the heroes mentioned so far who have overcome crippling

physical handicaps, all went on to more or less intellectual triumphs —in writing, painting, governing, and the like. But what of a young military flier and would-be warrior who is literally cut in half? Well, if he is Douglas Bader, he goes on to war, regardless. Douglas Bader was twenty-one, and a promising pilot in training at England's Royal Air Force College when, one day in 1931, while doing some tricky (and forbidden) aerobatics at "grass-cutting" low altitude, he plowed into the ground. He was hauled unconscious from the wreckage and woke up in a hospital with both legs gone. Bader could have retired right then, to live out his life on a disability pension and self-pity. He didn't. He was determined to stand on his own two feet —even if they had to be aluminum.

The enormity of Bader's injury must be explained. A man who loses *one* leg still has all the muscles, nerves and feeling in the remaining one; a tremendous advantage in maneuvering and counterbalancing the artificial other leg. Even Bader would not have been so terribly disabled if he had lost both legs below the knee; with thigh muscles and knee joints in both legs, even two artificial lower limbs can be managed fairly well. But Douglas Bader had only one knee. His left leg had been amputated at mid-calf. His right leg was amputated entire, very close to the hip.

His aluminum left leg comprised a foot jointed to a short metal calf whose leather socket fitted the stump of his own calf. Metal bars on each side of the leg hinged at his knee and ended in a leather band that laced around his thigh. This leg could be manipulated fairly normally by the action of his own thigh and knee muscles. His right leg, however, was artificial for its full length, jointed at "ankle" and "knee," ending in an artificial thigh that came right up to his groin and was held on by a broad leather corset around his abdomen. Thus, while Bader could "walk" his left leg, he could propel the right only by a jerk of his whole right side. Furthermore, he had to learn a whole new sense of balance, because the artificial legs, being much lighter than legs of flesh and bone, made him topheavy and unsteady.

But walk he did, though it took him months to learn. Every time he fell down, which he frequently did, just getting up again was equivalent to another man's climbing a cliff. He went on to learn to drive a car with special controls that were mostly worked by hand. Then he talked the Royal Air Force into letting him fly a plane again —which was actually easier than maneuvering a car, his feet and legs having much less to do. One of his superiors wrote, "When flying with this officer it is quite impossible to even imagine that he has two artificial legs. He is full of confidence and possesses excellent judgment and air sense. I have never met a more enthusiastic pilot. He lives for flying."

Nevertheless, in 1933, the RAF retired Bader for "reasons of health." He spent six years of frustration in a dreary civilian office job. Then, in September of 1939, the Second World War began. The Royal Air Force needed all the pilots it could get, and within two months Bader was back in the cockpit of a fighter plane. He even had one advantage over his flying mates. When he went to bed, he simply parked his legs alongside, with trousers, socks and shoes already on them. If his squadron got a sudden order to "scramble," he could be dressed for action in half the time it took his fellow pilots.

Bader shot down his first German plane in May of 1940. A month later, he was made leader of his squadron. In September of that year, he shot down his tenth and eleventh enemy planes, thus officially becoming an ace (in the RAF a pilot who has downed ten or more enemy planes). He was thenceforth known throughout the RAF— and to the Germans as well, who had heard of this fantastic pilot —as "the legless ace." In March of 1941, Bader was promoted to commander of a full wing of squadrons (equivalent to a U.S. Air Force officer rising in little more than one year from lieutenant to lieutenant-colonel).

Then, in a dogfight in August of 1941, his plane collided with a German plane at 24,000 feet, and its tail assembly was sheared off. Bader tried to bail out, but his right leg caught on something in the cockpit, and he found himself trapped as the plane drove earthward at 500 miles an hour. The artificial leg tore loose, and he was free to open his parachute. For the first time, he was thankful that he didn't have a real right leg, or he'd have ridden his plane right into the ground. He was lucky for another reason that the leg had ripped off. Landing by parachute is not like landing on a feather bed, it is like jumping off a twelve-foot wall. Had Bader landed on the stiff artificial leg, it might have skewered him.

He landed in occupied France, and was taken to a German military hospital. There he was visited by admiring German *Luftwaffe* pilots. "We are comrades on the wrong sides," they said, bringing him champagne and tobacco. They found the wreckage of his plane, and the mangled leg, and had it repaired for him. They showed him over their nearby airdrome, and even let him sit in the cockpit of one of their Messerschmitt fighters. Bader was practically unguarded in the hospital; who could expect such a cripple to escape? But he did, knotting bedsheets together and climbing down from his third-floor ward. He got a considerable distance across France before the Germans caught up with him, and then he was sent to a prison camp in Germany. He made several other attempts to escape, but none succeeded, and he remained a prisoner until the war was over.

During his career as "the legless ace," Bader downed twenty-two enemy planes, and was only the third man in British history to win both the Distinguished Service Order and the Distinguished Flying Cross, each of them twice. On September 15, 1945, three hundred RAF aircraft flew in mass formation over London to celebrate the end of the war. The fly-over was led by Group Captain Douglas Bader. After his discharge, Bader continued to fly, as a traveling troubleshooter for a worldwide oil corporation. In between flying the company plane on business missions, he has spent his spare time working with and encouraging—by his own example—other amputees and cripples.

CHRISTY BROWN

Writing is a difficult business under the best of circumstances. Hence one of my personal favorite heroes is an Irish writer. Christy Brown lives in Dublin, where he was born in 1932. He suffered brain damage at birth, and all his life he has been what doctors call an "athetoid." He has no control over his muscles; his head, fingers and limbs twitch or writhe almost continuously, sometimes his whole body at once. He cannot feed himself, nor dress himself, and of course he cannot walk. He gets about by wheelchair now, but in his early years his family was too poor to afford one. He got about indoors by crawling like an awkward baby, and outdoors by being pulled in a homemade wagon by his brothers. He has never been to school.

The brain damage he suffered was only to its motor functions, however, and not to the thinking part of his brain. He persevered for several years to learn to read, and, once he had learned, he read voraciously. Amazingly, his mother was able to teach him to write —because Christy does have conscious control over just one small part of his body: his left foot. Gripping a piece of chalk in the toes of this foot, he was able to begin scrawling letters, and then words, on the kitchen-floor linoleum. Dublin's Dr. Robert Collis taught

Christy certain remedial exercises calculated to still the constant movements of his body for welcome intervals of some duration, and also encouraged him to do what Christy had wanted to do, but never dreamed that he *could* do—to write for publication.

At twenty-two, he published *The Childhood Story of Christy Brown*. Patiently written on the floor, grueling word by word, phrase by phrase, sentence by sentence, and transcribed on a typewriter by his sister, the book was praised by critics, popular with readers, and earned Christy enough money so that the first luxury he bought for himself was an electric typewriter. No more writing on the floor with chalk or crayon; no more painfully slow transcribing. Now Christy types his own material himself—with his left big toe. Still, it took him seventeen more years to write his second book of autobiography, *Down All the Days*.

These books would rank as an heroic achievement against overwhelming odds even if they were only hackwork. But Christy Brown's writings have been rightly compared to those of such Irish masters as Sean O'Casey, J. M. Synge and even Ireland's great James Joyce. Christy Brown writes books that make other writers, like me, forget what agony went into every word of them, forget the terrible price Christy has paid for his talent, and make us mutter enviously to ourselves, "I wish I could have written that!"

Heroes of Our Times

A man does what he must—in spite of personal
consequences, in spite of obstacles and
dangers and pressures—and that is the basis
of all human morality.

—John F. Kennedy

WINSTON CHURCHILL

At the moment you are reading this, if Churchill were still alive, he would only recently have celebrated his 100th birthday. It's a wonder he didn't; he was a man of prodigious vitality. He died in his 91st year, and he was doing something worthy of notice and admiration during almost every one of those 91 years. Even a dispassionate encyclopedia article says of Churchill: "He is considered by many to have been the outstanding public figure of the twentieth century."

Winston Leonard Spencer Churchill was born in 1874. His father was an English lord and his mother was a famous American beauty —which is no bad way to start life. As a boy in the 1880's, Winston was a scapegrace, noted mainly for mischief and an aversion to study, so that he barely scraped through his early schools. His father, a distinguished Member of Parliament, despaired of Winston's ever following him into those august halls, and so enlisted the boy in the Royal Military College (better known as Sandhurst military

197

academy). Winston graduated into the Royal Army just in time to go off to service in a frontier war in India. As a very junior officer and the son of a *Very Important Person*, he could easily have remained obscure and safely out of combat, but instead he boldly made his way to the very front lines and (ofttimes against orders) performed daring (read foolhardy) heroics which got him "mentioned in dispatches," and his name began to be noticed.

To make sure that his name was noticed, he came home and wrote two brilliant books about the Indian campaigns which rather criticized the conduct of the war, and he fell into disfavor with his superior officers. When the South African War broke out in 1899, those officers made sure Churchill was not assigned to take part. He was determined to get into the fracas, however, and arranged with a London newspaper to go as a war correspondent. Because he was always in the thick of the fighting, and, indeed, did a good deal of it himself, eventually he was captured by the Dutch Boers. He made a spectacular escape from a prison camp and this time his name did make the newspaper headlines in England. With delight, the English people followed the accounts of how Churchill was eluding the Boers' search for him over all South Africa. (Churchill was ever afterward peeved because the Boers put up such a paltry reward—£50 —for his capture.)

Churchill came back to England a popular hero and, on the strength of that popularity, was elected to Parliament at the tender age of twenty-six. He served in several government appointments, and by 1911 was First Lord of the Admiralty. Under Churchill, the Royal Navy saw the introduction of the 15-inch gun (biggest of its time), the super-fast "Queen Elizabeth" type of battleship, and the first light cruisers. In 1914 the First World War broke out, and Churchill's Navy performed beautifully, clearing the seas of German warships—until, in 1915, an English naval expedition suffered a crushing defeat in the Dardanelles. Churchill was blamed and dismissed from office.

Churchill put on his Army uniform again and went off to active service in France. Two years later, he was recalled to government duties, variously in charge of air power and munitions. In the latter office, he oversaw the development of a brand-new secret weapon. To disguise its nature while it was being worked on, the various components were always shipped in big crates which Churchill ordered marked simply "tank." Thus, the awesome war weapon is still known by that rather nondescript name.

Despite Churchill's contributions to winning the war, he was afterward shunted into obscure offices. He had already performed enough heroic deeds to satisfy the ordinary man for a lifetime, but he felt crushed that his public career seemed to be over. He spent twenty years in relative oblivion—and chafing at it—devoting his time to writing, painting and lecturing. He published distinguished books on the First World War and a couple of not very good novels. By the early 1930's, he was making speeches against a new threat from Germany in the form of a rising young leader named Adolf Hitler. But Churchill was ignored; with most Englishmen regarding Hitler as a harmless pipsqueak.

As we know, they were proved wrong. In 1939, Hitler launched the most devastating war the world has seen. Churchill, who had early foreseen the danger, was called to the helm of the ship of state as Prime Minister of England—and he was to become the greatest premier England has ever known. On taking office, he said, "I have nothing to offer but blood, toil, tears and sweat." He was a consummate leader and organizer of the war effort, however, whose speeches alone were enough to inspire Britons to unbelievable heroic resistance. In 1940, when the rest of its allies in Western Europe had surrendered to Hitler, and England stood alone against the mighty Nazi war machine, expecting invasion at any moment, Churchill declaimed:

"We shall defend our island, whatever the cost may be; we shall fight on the beaches, we shall fight on the landing grounds, we shall fight in the fields and in the streets, we shall fight in the hills; we shall never surrender." And later: "Let us therefore brace ourselves that, if the British Empire and its Commonwealth last for a thousand years, men will still say, 'This was their finest hour.'"

When the Second World War was finally won, Churchill was one of the dominant forces in forging the peace terms and unscrambling the mess Hitler had made of the European countries' borders. Churchill foresaw and warned against the growing menace of the Soviet Union's land grabs (it was he who popularized the term "Iron Curtain"). He originated the idea of "summit conferences" directly between heads of nations, rather than between their underling ambassadors. He went on writing superb histories almost to the end of his life, and in 1953 won the Nobel Prize for Literature. In the same year, Queen Elizabeth II conferred a knighthood upon him. In 1963, U.S. President Kennedy granted honorary American citizenship to the old warrior.

When Churchill died in 1965, his funeral, the most splendid of the century, was attended by the kings and presidents of almost every major nation in the world. Millions of words were written and spoken in obituary praise of him. But Churchill had already spoken, twenty-five years earlier, what could well be his most fitting epitaph: "We must all thank God that we have been allowed, each of us according to our stations, to play a part in making these days memorable in the history of our race."

MAO TSE-TUNG

When Winston Churchill spoke of "our race," he referred to the nations of English-speaking peoples. But there is another and far more numerous "race" on earth. (Actually, there is only one *human race* inhabiting the planet, but we often speak of "the yellow race" when referring to the Chinese.) And the Chinese have a warrior-statesman-hero of their own, whom they revere quite as much as we do a Churchill. He is China's "Chairman" Mao Tse-tung.

Mao has long detested the capitalistic policies of the western world, and the West in turn has despised his communism, which makes us and his Communist Chinese regard each other as real or potential enemies. Nevertheless, Mao Tse-tung is a hero to the 700,-000,000 Chinese. A book on heroes can hardly ignore a man who is regarded as almost godlike by one-fifth of the world's population.

Mao is in his eighties, however, and in failing health, and may be dead by the time you read this. But his memory is certain to be enshrined by the Chinese, as we have enshrined the memory of Lincoln and Churchill. The "little red book," *The Thoughts of Chairman Mao*, is practically the Bible of every Communist Chinese, and is sure to be so for generations, if not for ages.

Undeniably, in his younger years, Mao did personal deeds of true heroism. It was as recently as 1912 that China dethroned its last despotic emperor. Though it declared itself a republic, it was actually a war ground of numerous factions fighting for control of the country—among them the Nationalists and the Communists. The Communists were far outnumbered, poorly equipped, and constantly persecuted. In 1927 there was a mass assassination of them by the Nationalists. The remaining few, mostly country peasants, would have been butchered as well, had not Mao Tse-tung led them on the famous "Long March" to safety.

Without a single wheeled vehicle, Mao led his patchwork guerrilla band trudging across more than 6,000 miles of wild country—and through ten different Nationalist armies, one after the other. In all, the Communists crossed eighteen mountain ranges and twenty-four rivers, fought at least one battle a day against their harassers, until they set up a stronghold in the impregnable mountains of northwest China. They emerged in 1937, when the Japanese invaded China, to fight shoulder to shoulder with the Nationalist armies against their common enemy. That war went on to blend into the Second World War. By the time it had ended, the Communists had become the strongest party in China and soon took over entirely. Mao Tse-tung has been Chairman (read "dictator") since 1949.

Any Communist country is a society where, as novelist T. H. White put it, "Everything that is not forbidden is compulsory." But it cannot be denied that, under Mao, the Chinese have lived and thrived better and more happily than they ever did in their centuries of rule by khans, emperors, warlords and petty tyrants. Also, in recent years Mao and his administration have seemed increasingly receptive to friendly gestures from the West—trade agreements and cultural exchanges. We don't have to embrace Communism or even admire it, but perhaps the Chinese will not be our "enemies" forever.

ALEKSANDR SOLZHENITSYN

Communism is a political system of harsh suppression of personal liberties, of censorship and thought control—and that very fact has created another hero of our times, Aleksandr Solzhenitsyn. He is a writer who loves his "Mother Russia" with a passion, and who has become one of her most famous sons. But the Soviet Union has hardly reciprocated that love. It has treated Solzhenitsyn most disgracefully. As a young man, and fiercely patriotic, Solzhenitsyn fought for his country with distinction in the Second World War. Then, in a 1945 letter to a friend, he made an indiscreet reference to "the man with the mustache"—meaning dictator Josef Stalin—and the letter was intercepted by a military censor. That no-worse-than-foolish remark about "the man with the mustache" doomed Aleksandr Solzhenitsyn to eight years' hard labor in prison. Even after he had served his sentence, he was exiled to a labor camp in far Siberia for three more years, and was not freed until 1956.

By that time, Stalin was dead, and had been discredited and reviled by his successors in power. So there was no official complaint when in 1962 Solzhenitsyn published a book called *One Day in the*

Life of Ivan Denisovich, detailing some of the horrors he had suffered as a result of Stalin's cruel dictatorship. The novel was published both in the Soviet Union and abroad, and won him immediate international fame. It was all right for Solzhenitsyn to write denunciations of the now-hated Stalin. Then he began to write novels equally critical of the present government, and he was refused permission to publish them. So he smuggled the manuscripts out of the Soviet Union—such books as *The First Circle* and *Cancer Ward*—and they were published in other countries. His reputation continued to grow, around the world. He was Russia's greatest writer since Tolstoy—which is the equivalent of saying that an English writer is the greatest since Shakespeare—and his countrymen were forbidden to read anything he wrote. Indeed, Solzhenitsyn lived from day to day in expectation of being again arrested for his "treasonous" acts of smuggling his works out of Russia.

The Free World at least gave him due recognition. In 1970, he was awarded the Nobel Prize for Literature, but Solzhenitsyn declined to travel to Sweden to accept the prize, for fear that the

Soviet authorities would forbid his re-entering his beloved Russia. Solzhenitsyn did, however, send an acceptance speech, and in it he boldly proclaimed that "Man's salvation lies in everyone making it his business to know everything"—a sentiment not calculated to please the repressive and secretive government of his own country. From then on, he was practically under house arrest: his every movement followed, his every action monitored, and his every writing still banned from publication there.

Solzhenitsyn heroically continued to write what he felt had to be said. In 1974, he somehow smuggled out of the country his most scathing denunciation of the Communist regime—*The Gulag Archipelago*—and he truly did expect the secret police at his door. But he was by then such a towering international figure that even the enraged Soviet government realized it could not again imprison this man without raising an outcry around the world. Instead, Solzhenitsyn was ordered to leave the country.

Solzhenitsyn is such a devout Russian that he would probably have preferred even Siberian exile again, if only he could remain a citizen. "All my life is here," he once said. "I listen only to Russia's sadness; I write only about it." But leave he had to, and he now makes his home in Switzerland. This was perhaps the greatest sacrifice he could have made on behalf of his work. But Russia's loss is the Free World's gain. From now on, we will have much easier access to Aleksandr Solzhenitsyn's heroic writings.

Martin Luther King

The imperfections of Communist Russia and Communist China may be more evident, but that doesn't mean that the leading country of the Free World—the United States of America—is perfect and beyond need for improvement. The United States has long oppressed, segregated and discriminated against many of its minority inhabitants, most notably the blacks. In the 1950's, a considerable number of blacks rebelled against this oppression, foremost among them a young Negro minister, the Reverend Doctor Martin Luther King.

King was no fiery-eyed revolutionary. He had no plans for planting bombs or hijacking airplanes, or any of the other violent tactics that later terrorist groups adopted. He had studied the "passive resistance" policies of Mohandas Gandhi, and he conducted his black civil rights revolution absolutely peacefully. In those days, in the Southern states—among numerous other humiliations—Negroes were forced to ride in the back seats of city busses. King preached, "Brothers and sisters, don't ride in the busses at all," and they didn't. Blacks who had automobiles formed car pools; others walked. The bus companies suddenly discovered they were losing money. White passengers still arrogantly rode in the front seats, but there weren't enough of them to pay the companies to operate. It wasn't long before the transit companies abandoned the "back of the bus" policy; a Negro passenger could ride in whatever seat he chose.

That was the opening wedge. Next, Martin Luther King arranged "sit-ins" in all-white restaurants that had refused to serve blacks. Negroes simply went in and sat at the tables, in booths or on counter stools . . . and waited. The restaurants refused to serve them, and often evicted them. But the blacks were breaking no law; all they did was sit. And they continued to sit patiently in those places until, one after another, the restaurants capitulated and began to serve them. White patrons eventually got used to seeing blacks eating at other tables, while the restaurant owners were both surprised and pleased to find that their "surrender" actually meant a rise in patronage and profits.

Black comedian and civil rights campaigner Dick Gregory has a favorite story of this period. He said, "I sat at this one counter for six months before they agreed to serve me. And then they didn't have anything I wanted."

Martin Luther King went on to arrange other peaceable marches and demonstrations. These were often broken up by white policemen using fire hoses, vicious dogs, truncheons and guns. But King urged his people not to fight back or even defend themselves. There were in those days more heroes than one can count—including innumerable blacks (and white sympathizers and co-marchers) who were shot, stabbed or beaten to death by "white supremacy" bigots.

Martin Luther King and his followers prevailed. Conditions are still far from ideal for the Negro in America—in the South or North —but the civil rights movement forced new laws, from the Federal level down to the municipal, granting rights, privileges, liberties and justice which the Negro had never known before. The sweeping civil-rights laws likewise benefited other minorities, such as the Chicanos (Mexican-Americans) and Puerto Ricans. And King's successful tactics have since inspired many other "second-class citizens"— including women—to stand up and demand equality of job opportunity, equal pay for equal labor, and other rights that should have been granted long ago.

In 1964, in recognition of his contributions to humanity, the Rev. Dr. King was awarded the Nobel Peace Prize. He was only the second black American to receive that supreme award (UN ambassador Ralph Bunche was the first, in 1950), and King was the youngest man, at thirty-five, ever to receive that honor.

Four years later, Dr. King was shot down from cowardly ambush by a fanatical white racist. His life had been heroic, and it ended in heroic martyrdom. If I were a black, I would like to remember Martin Luther King with the words once applied to a soldier who died untimely young: "He gave us everything he never had."

POPE JOHN XXIII

It may be difficult, at first encounter, to conceive of a lofty, remote and well-cushioned church prelate as "heroic." But Pope John XXIII certainly was one of the most beloved men of our time—not only was he loved by the 600,000,000 Roman Catholics of whom he was spiritual leader but also by people of other faiths and even no

206 Mark of the Heroes

206 March of the Heroes

faith. And he did effect some changes in his church which took considerable heroism, in that he opposed many crusty old church officials in order to update attitudes and policies made iron-clad by the venerability of hundreds of years of existence.

The future Pope John was born plain Angelo Roncalli, son of a poor peasant farmer in the hill country of northern Italy. Throughout his life, though his work and travels made him intimate with kings, presidents and other notables, he maintained his peasant humility. His predecessor on the papal throne, Pius XII, had used his high position to advance the fortunes of his innumerable kinfolk. But John XXIII said of his own kin—even his poor farmer brothers—"They are the relatives of the pope. They dine with me once a year. That should be enough for them."

The young Angelo was such a bright child that he impressed the Italian noble for whom his father farmed. It was that gentleman who arranged and paid for his schooling, and eventually saw to it that he went on to the seminary. After his ordination, Roncalli's earliest priestly assignments were fairly obscure—he taught at the seminary from which he had graduated, he was a chaplain in the Italian Army during the First World War—but he performed these duties with sufficient distinction and dedication to bring him to the notice of the Vatican, and from that time on his rise in the church was rapid.

As a papal nuncio, variously stationed in Bulgaria, France, and Turkey, he was a sort of roving troubleshooter for the church. In this quasi-diplomatic office, he quietly arranged informal but quite productive meetings among the various ambassadors of almost all the nations of Europe, and did more to keep peace among those nations than has ever been told. When the Second World War did erupt, Archbishop Roncalli was stationed in Turkey, and helped thousands of Jews escape through that country from Hitler's domains. Once, when a consignment of some four hundred small Jewish children had been smuggled out of Germany without passports or papers of any sort, petty officialdom refused them permission to travel to their destination of Palestine. Roncalli took it upon himself to baptize every one of them a "temporary Roman Catholic," so that he could give them papers bearing his own visa and they could go on to safety.

It was not until he was elected pope, in 1958, that John XXIII was able to realize his long-cherished ambition. He convoked the second Ecumenical Council in the history of the church. ("Ecumenical" refers to worldwide church activities, especially in respect to Christian unity.) The first and only previous such council had been held nearly one hundred years before, and confined to Roman Catholics. This time—and here he broke tradition and ruffled many Vatican elders—Pope John invited many non-Catholic delegates as observers. Ever since the Reformation, the Roman Catholic and its sister church, the Greek Orthodox, had stood aloof from the Protestant faiths (and indeed, to some extent from each other). Now Pope John called a council to promote unity among *all* Christian faiths. That council did relax a number of doctrinal rigidities. Protestants were no longer to be regarded as out-and-out infidels, automatically damned. Though Pope John died shortly afterward—in 1963, at the age of eighty-one—his work has survived him. The Roman Catholic Church has continued in many ways to modernize and unbend and reshape its attitudes more in line with today's world, as John had wanted.

Earlier I referred to a "lofty, remote" church prelate. Most popes are just that, but John never was; he was touchingly and openly charming. In 1962, he granted a private audience to the wife of President Kennedy, and wondered beforehand exactly how he should address her. An adviser told him, "The Americans call her simply Mrs. Kennedy, but since she is of French descent and you will be speaking that language, you might call her Madame." John tried it different ways: "Mrs. Kennedy . . . Madame Kennedy . . . Madame." But when she appeared in his doorway—young, beautiful, demure—the old man simply spread his arms wide, beamed, and welcomed her warmly with "Jacqueline!"

MOON LANDING

Most of the heroic adventures of the past were accomplished by some man or woman or group, alone on the high seas or in a jungle or on an icecap or some other frontier far from the eyes of civilization. The most heroic adventure of our own time, however, was watched and heard by millions of people all over the world via the medium of television. Perhaps you, too, eavesdropped on the event. It happened at 10:56 P.M., Eastern Daylight Time, on July 20, 1969. Listen:

HOUSTON CONTROL: You are *go* for landing. Over.
EAGLE: Roger, *go* for landing. Three thousand feet. We're go. We're go.
HOUSTON: *Eagle*, looking great. You're *go*.

EAGLE: Lights on. Down two and a half. Forward, forward forty feet, down two and a half. Picking up some dust. Thirty feet, two and a half down shadow, four forward. Four forward, drifting to the right a little.

HOUSTON: Thirty seconds.

EAGLE: Contact light. Okay, engines stop. Engine arm off.

HOUSTON: We copy. You're down, *Eagle*.

EAGLE: Houston, Tranquility Base here. The *Eagle* has landed.

The *Eagle* was the first moon lander to carry men. A few minutes after that exchange, an astronaut stepped from the *Eagle*'s ladder onto the surface of the moon, with the historic remark: "That's one small step for a man, one giant leap for mankind."

The first man on the moon was 38-year-old Neil Armstrong, though it could have been any other of America's thirty-two astronauts. They were all identically selected, tested and trained to perform any space mission they might be assigned. It just happened to be Armstrong's turn to command this Apollo 11 flight. He had already been into space before, orbiting the earth in Gemini 8. His two Apollo 11 flight mates, Michael Collins and Edwin Aldrin, had also been into space before. So had twenty other American astronauts and sixteen Russian cosmonauts (including one woman).

Neil Armstrong is almost the prototype of the "all-American hero." As an Ohio small-town boy, he'd taken his first plane ride at the age of six, in an old Ford trimotor plane, and thereafter he had been obsessed with flying. At age seven, cutting grass in a cemetery for ten cents an hour, he spent each dime to buy a balsa-wood model airplane kit. He left college to become a U.S. Navy pilot, and flew seventy-eight combat missions during the Korean War. After his discharge from the Navy, he became a civilian test pilot. In 1962, he was the first non-military pilot accepted for NASA's astronaut corps. When he made his first space flight aboard Gemini 8, that craft's automatic guidance system went wild and threw the space capsule rolling and tumbling out of control. Calmly, Armstrong took over the manual controls, stabilized the bucking craft, and thus saved the lives of himself and his co-pilot. Neil Armstrong was authentically of heroic caliber.

A lot of people have tried to downgrade his achievement in being the first man to walk on the moon. They have pointed out that really it was just "his turn." They have pointed out that he could never have made the voyage without the back-up efforts of 20,000

industrial contractors, scores of university laboratories, a total of 400,000 people working in the space program—and an expenditure of 25½ billion dollars, counting all the trial flights that had gone before. Armstrong's space suit and life-support apparatus alone cost two million dollars. (By contrast, Lindbergh spent $15,000 to make his historic first solo flight across the Atlantic. Lewis and Clark made their expedition from St. Louis to the Pacific and back on only $2,500 worth of supplies.)

Neil Armstrong may have been no braver than any of his fellow astronauts, just luckier in his assignment. But no amount of caviling can take away from him that achievement or his assured place in history. No matter how much more space-traveling men may do, whether to other planets in our own solar system or perhaps someday to other planetary systems, even to other galaxies, this fact will remain forever. Neil Armstrong was the first human being ever to step from the planet Earth to another sphere in space.

I can't begin to list the many other men and women whom I consider heroes of our times, much less those thousands of the past whom I have neglected to include. But in some future edition of this book, I might like to add a chapter called *The Heroes of Tomorrow*, and I would be grateful for suggestions as to whom I should include. As we have seen, a hero must stand the test of time. Just as we never know whether a book, a painting or a piece of music can be considered a "classic" until it has survived and been remembered and praised for years or generations, so it is with a hero, who may be a worldwide celebrity today and forgotten tomorrow.

You might write and let me know whether you consider one or more of these individuals of today and yesterday as a hero whose memory will survive: the late UN secretary-general Dag Hammarskjold; American diplomat Henry Kissinger; German's "rebuilder" Konrad Adenauer; France's warrior-statesman Charles de Gaulle; Israel's founding father David Ben-Gurion or recent prime minister Mrs. Golda Meir; English peace-campaigner Bertrand Russell; American writer-adventurer Ernest Hemingway; black American athlete Willie Mays or Hank Aaron; some other sports great; noted evangelist Dr. Billy Graham; space-flight pioneer Wernher von Braun; polio-vaccine discoverer Dr. Jonas Salk, and on and on. Doubtless you can think of other candidates, perhaps authentic heroes, of whom I am unaware.

INDEX OF NAMES

INDEX OF NAMES